INDEX

FOREWARD

BY: TONY GREENLAND

As I approach my seventieth Birthday I feel honored that not only that I should be remembered by Adam, but that I should also write the forward to his publication(s)

It was some twenty years ago that from writing articles in modelling magazines around the world I was asked to write a book with the rather grandiose title "Panzer Modelling Masterclass". At this time I believed it was generally well received and I made an attempt to cover all facets of modelling a tank (be it always a German WWII model!). My emphasis was very much on Kit Improvement and alterations to produce as accurate a kit in all aspects. From construction, decals, painting to the theater of operations.

The overriding necessity to improve the kit slowly became redundant as the likes of Dragon, Trumpeter, AFV club, etc , etc began releasing highly accurate kits. To me the painting was but one of the stages in production. All too often when criticized for too "pretty" a model I used the excuse of "the model represents the actual vehicle and not the Battle or Country it fought in". The book was successful if the reviews are to be believed, but, one would need to be very conceited to believe that the zenith had been reached. If you write a book

about techniques (...on any subject) there will always be someone out there that reads your work and who will pick up the baton and improve upon what you may have considered as your unique technique.

Since those halcyon days of the 1990's I have observed a distinct change in the emphasis in the AFV modelling world. There are a substantial number of highly talented finishers of these high quality kits. The emphasis has changed from construction to finishing. The quality of the kits and the finishing is breathtaking in their realism. A consequence of these finishing styles is the plethora of paints/pigments available to the modeller that bring such realism to their model. With these products are a large number of publications on "how to do". Why are these two volumes from Adam different from other publications? Well, together they cover the full spectrum of modelling AFV's. Every aspect of modelling AFV's is treated in a professional, readable and easily understood manner. The purchase of these two publications would provide a lifetime of information to build and improve upon even the most talented modeller, no longer just the finishing but all aspect of construction to completion.

1 INTRODUCTION & ACKNOWLEDGMENTS

INTRODUCTION

THIS IS A PROJECT THAT I HAVE BEEN WORKING ON INTERMITTENTLY FOR ABOUT EIGHT YEARS.

These two books cover everything that I have learned, studied and taught myself about building and painting Armour Models. There are many step-by-step photos to aid in the explanation of the methods covered. As I said in the intro of the first book, it is important that you also read the text in order to obtain a good understanding of the various techniques explained. Viewers do not always take the time to carefully read everything focusing only on the photos. As a result they do not always obtain all of the information that is available.

These two books cover in detail the construction and painting phases in order performed by myself and many other modellers throughout the completion of a scale armour model. The first book includes examples of everything from choosing a subject along with different examples of basic construction methods up to cleaning and assembling resin parts and soldering photo etched brass. In this second book, I cover the painting phases in equal detail again using different examples. Applying basecoats through to various paint chipping methods are demonstrated along with different examples and methods of weathering. These books are not just about different techniques but also concerning how to use them together to obtain authentic looking results. You will see in many examples that numerous techniques look best when combined with other methods, therefore many techniques will be demonstrated in various examples throughout different chapters. Learning different techniques is only one thing. The important thing is understanding when and how to use combinations of these techniques together that is the true secret to obtaining realistic finishes.

This second book will cover all of the painting and weathering methods in the order that they are usualy carried out when finishing an AFV model. It is important to realise that the application of these steps can sometimes vary depending on the subject. You do not always need to rely on a specific order or sequence of techniques but more on the techniques you have at your disposal. I will start now by explaining a bit about what I consider when choosing a theme for painting an armour model.

ACKNOWLEDGMENTS

THE FOLLOWING HAVE CONTRIBUTED, ADVISED AND ENCOURAGED ME DURING THE MAKING OF THESE TWO BOOKS.

I would like to thank Thomas Anderson and Daniele Guglielmi for the historical photos. I would also like to express my gratitude to Sven Frisch along with Gail and Jeff Wilder for their continual counsel and also helping with the text of both books. Jari Hemila for the step-by-step photos in the segment about applying markings and Insignia is also much appreciated. I would like to thank Sven Frisch, Harry Steinmüller and Scott Negron for the information and assistance with the Zimmerit Chapter. Thanks to the people at Lifecolor, Valljo Acrylics and Aber for the consumables and parts needed to finish the models seen throughout these pages. Finally I would like to thank Ivan Cocker, César Oliva and Calvin Tan for the wonderful figures seen throughout these pages.

I WOULD ALSO LIKE TO THANK THE FOLLOWING FOR THEIR ADVICE AND SUPPORT THROUGHOUT THIS PROJECT.

David Parker
Keith Smith
Rodion Zotov
Maxim Chekanov, aka: Comanche75
Andrew Beletz
Francois Verdier

Jim Galante
Vladimir Yashin
Karl Logan
Zachary Vincentsex

HOW I APPROACH PAINTING AN AFV

MOST OF US KNOW HOW BUSY LIFE CAN GET. WE ALL DREAM ABOUT THE MANY SUBJECTS THAT WE WOULD LIKE TO FINISH BUT ONLY USUALLY END UP COMPLETING A FRACTION OF THEM.

Therefore we must choose which subjects are most important and focus on them if anything is going to get completed. I have been publishing for around ten years now. There are a number of things that I always consider prior to making a model. I am normally not a scratch-builder so those factors are largely to do with how the model is going to be painted.

As a professional I begin by thinking about if the model is a common subject or not. Has it been completed well by other modellers and published recently in magazines or on a well known webpage? If it has, can I then paint this model with an unusual theme or maybe using a different set of finishing techniques that have not been published in order to set it apart from the others?

Other very important things that I consider are if it will challenge me. Will I enjoy painting it? A lot of the subjects that I have published are just AFVs that I wanted to see finished in a specific way or simply have not seen modeled before. I also consider what the overall shape and colour of the model is going to look like. Does it have interesting textures and details that will be fun to paint? Will it photograph nicely after it's finished? I carefully consider all of this prior to undertaking and/or committing to any new projects.

After deciding to commit to a project there are still a number of things to consider. One is if the model is going to have an intricate camouflage or not. A camouflage will help me to decide if it might not be within my best interest to apply the Colour Modulation style.

I also think about how much weathering do I want the completed subject to have? If the model is only going to have light weathering I will need to depend more on methods such as blending oils along with chipping and rust effects to create contrast amongst the different details. If the model is going to be weathered heavily I will be able to create contrast amongst parts largely using dust and other earth effects. Effectively creating contrast is very important.

CREATING CONTRAST BETWEEN DETAILS (DISTINCTION METHOD)

BEING ABLE TO CREATE CONTRAST BETWEEN THE VARIOUS DETAILS OF A MODEL IS A VERY SIGNIFICANT SKILL TO HAVE .

I will demonstrate this numerous times throughout this book. Contrast helps to separate and draw attention to the different parts of a replica. A well painted model will contain lots of contrast between the different parts making it so much more interesting to look at. The trick to creating contrast is to do so without making it look obvious. I have been loosely referring to this style as "The Distinction Method". In fact it also encompasses Color Modulation. Let's look at a few examples before we get started.

PHOTO 1

Along with exaggerating volumes the Colour Modulation Style is also about creating contrast amongst details. The lighter green gradient shifting toward the lower part of the turret of the KV-1 helps to distinguish it from the upper hull. Note the lighter straps securing the cylindrical fuel tank as well as the flame cut ages on the top of the turret casting distinguishing it from the upper plate. The same goes for the upper ends of the hull side plates.

01

PHOTO 2:
The Colour Modulation is less obvious on the completed KV-1 but the contrast that I pointed out between the parts is still evident. The washes, chipping and earth tones have all helped to tone the contrast down a little. Again, the trick is to know how to make the contrast effective without making it obvious. Also evident in this photo is how the weathering plays a role in conjunction with Colour Modulation. One area where we can clearly see this is with the dark moist satin earth tones in the corners distinguishing the fender, hull and triangular fender supports from each other.

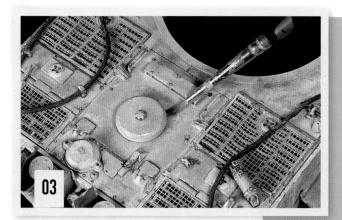

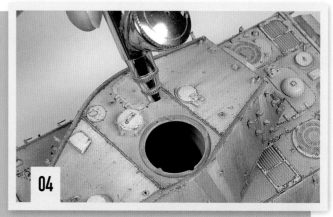

PHOTO 3 THROUGH 5:
Creating contrast amongst details can simply be done by brushing light earth coloured pigments around them as on the rear armoured vent of this Tiger I or the cupola on the E-75. Wet-effects were also added over the dust tones to further enhance the effect as seen in the photo of the completed E-75.

PHOTO 6 THROUGH 8:
Larger subjects such as this 30,5cm SFL Bär often contain less weathering therefore other methods need to be relied on to distinguish parts from one another. On this example, oil paints and chipping effects were used for this task. Note the yellow oil paint blended onto the outer sides of the superstructure to help distinguish it from the top and rear plates. The washes applied to the flame cut edges and the paint chips refined to these interlocking corners also work in conjunction with the blended yellow oils. Different tones can also be seen amongst the various panels on the upper hull along with chipping effects distinguishing these parts from one another. Light weathering techniques can be used to make these effects less obvious resulting in a natural looking finish.

06

07

08

PHOTO 9:
Hare are a few more examples of using weathering to create contrast amongst different details. You can see the dark earth tones on the hull around the fender of this T-34. Note the lighter rust tones on the ends of the spare track distinguishing each of the links from one another.

PHOTO 10:
Effects like spilt fuel and grease can add contrast between parts. Here they are distinguishing the hull and fenders from each other. Some of the spilt fuel was placed onto the fender making the effect less obvious and more natural looking.

PHOTO 11 THROUGH 12:
The bedspring armour on the upper hull of this theoretical JS-3 has a number of various effects distinguishing the different parts. These effects were the light rust tones at the intersections of the frames and the chipped yellow civilian paint on a few of the lengths of angle bars.

09

10

Having a bit of an imagination with your choice of subjects can be the best way to help you distinguish different details as seen on the E-50 below. The different types of primer seen on the black fenders and light grey armoured covers protecting the exhausts easily distinguish these details from the red oxide hull.

Having an idea of how to use all of the methods highlighted in these photos to create contrast will allow you to draw attention to certain details. Furthermore your models will be more interesting as a whole making each of the parts more attractive both capturing and keeping the attention of viewers. This is why I refer to painting in this manner as "The Distinction Method" because Color Modulation is not always needed. Most of all, you will also discover that panting a model in this manner is much more enjoyable. Again, these painting methods will all be covered later, so let's get started with the basics of airbrushing, applying basecoats and painting camouflages.

11

12

03 APPLYING BASECOATS AND CAMOUFLAGES

THE FIRST LAYER OF PAINT THAT YOU APPLY ONTO A SCALE MODEL IS OFTEN REFERRED TO AS A BASE COAT.

This base colour serves as the pedestal that will work in conjunction with all of the following semi-transparent weathering steps and effects applied over it. Therefore the colour that you choose for a basecoat is very important as it will be altered by the subsequent finishing steps. The base coat also needs to be applied properly so it is smooth, without flaws and not hiding any of the important fine details while evenly covering the model. Of course much of the same goes for the camouflage that is usually applied immediately after.

The dark green shade airbrushed onto this JSU-152 is a good example of planning ahead when choosing your base colour. I mixed this tone to be rather light while also adding a lot of yellow for vibrancy. You will see throughout the next parts of this book that the lighter tone will be darkened to more of an accurate Russian green shade while still containing a hint of vitality after the washes, fading and other various weathering effects have been added.

Using a paintbrush for applying a basecoat is certainly an option although most hobbyists usually airbrush both the basecoat and the camouflage. Therefore airbrushing is vital to scale modelling and it's something that comes with practice. Properly maintaining your airbrush is very important in order to keep it functioning properly. Choosing your paints is also essential.

Over time you will also begin to find which paints you are most comfortable with when airbrushing.

These segments will contain information and examples for properly using and maintaining an airbrush. I will also discuss the methods and paints that I use to apply base coats and camouflages. These techniques are what I have learnt from experience over the years to get the results on the models that I publish. Let's now look at some things to keep in mind when purchasing an airbrush and compressor that will best fit your needs.

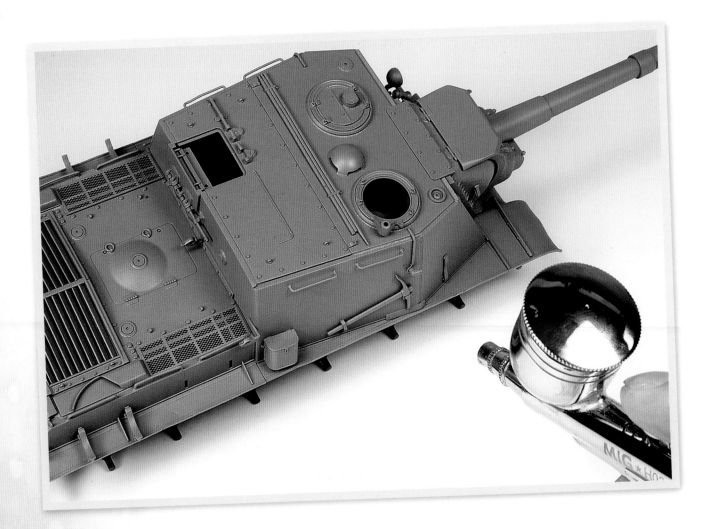

CHOOSING AN AIRBRUSH AND COMPRESSOR

ARGUABLY THE AIRBRUSH IS OUR MOST IMPORTANT TOOL WHEN IT COMES TO PAINTING REPLICAS.

Double action airbrushes are more or less the standard type used throughout the hobby. There are also single action type airbrushes but you cannot simultaneously control the airflow together with the amount of paint passing through the nozzle. This can be limiting when spraying camouflages or applying colour modulation for example. Although more expensive, a double action airbrush allows you to control both the amount of paint going through the nozzle and the airflow making it much more applicable for effectivly carrying out these tasks.

There is a wide range of airbrushes available in regards to both price and quality. One might think that professional modellers own a wide range of expensive airbrushes. In fact many practiced hobbyists still prefer their first airbrush which they have been comfortable with using for many years. With the exception of occasionally

replacing a part, purchasing a quality airbrush is an investment that you will only need to make once if you both take care of and clean it regularly. Most quality airbrushes also come with a warranty therefore you will be able to get most broken parts replaced for free.

An important factor with an airbrush is the width of the needle and its nozzle. Needles usually range from 0.2mm to 0.5mm. Smaller needles are suitable for very fine controlled camouflages and effects while bigger ones are better for larger surfaces such as applying base coats. Most good airbrushes are available in a choice of different sizes.

With a double action airbrush you can control the amount of paint that you are spraying onto the model. Therefore when using one you are less likely to encounter problems when quickly painting a large surface with a 0.2mm needle. With a single action type you might have difficulties when trying to spray very thin lines through a 0.5mm nozzle. Consequently if you are looking for an all-purpose scale modelling airbrush, a double action model containing a smaller nozzle is recommended.

With a bit of research and searching you should be able to find a good airbrush that fits your needs at a reasonable price lasting you for years to come. Remember that a little investment will most likely pay back in regards of quality, durability and therefore longevity. After you have purchased your airbrush the essential thing that you will need is experience, that can only be gained with practice. With experience you will also find that you are more comfortable with airbrushing some types of paint than others. Understanding the paints you use and how much to thin each of them for different types of finishes and effects will also come with practice allowing you to get the most out of your airbrush.

PHOTO 1:
These are the three airbrushes that I will be using throughout this book. They are all double action types. I have had the top Mig Productions airbrush containing a large cup for around six years now. This airbrush has a 0.3 nozzle allowing it to spray larger amounts of paint. It is ideal for quickly applying sound basecoats over larger subjects.

The middle one is a Tamiya superfine HG-SF model. It is a good general purpose airbrush containing a smaller 0.2mm nozzle. This was the only airbrush that I used for all of the articles that I published for almost seven years.

The bottom airbrush is an Infinity model by Harder and Steinbach. I only take it out when applying complexed camouflages and colour modulation. It was given to me as a gift a few years ago and I was initially discouraged with this model when I started using it. The action was different from the Tamiya superfine that I was accustomed to. After some time I was able to get familiar with the action of the Infinity and now consider to be the finest airbrush that I currently own.

Therefore, as I mentioned earlier, only with time and practice can you get accustomed to your airbrush allowing you to get the most out of it.

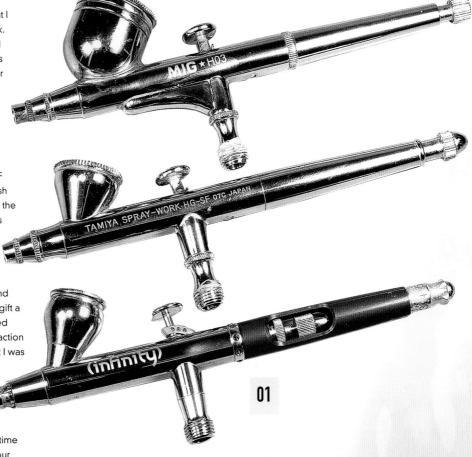

01

PHOTO 2:

The first thing that you should do upon purchasing an airbrush is disassemble it. Knowing how it goes together will give you and understanding of how it operates. Knowing how your airbrush functions will also allow you to quickly troubleshoot and clean it during and after use. We will discuss more about cleaning your airbrush shortly.

Your airbrush will also need a source of air in order to operate. There are also many different compressors available that differ in types and price. Like when looking for an airbrush you will want to do a bit of research before purchasing a compressor.

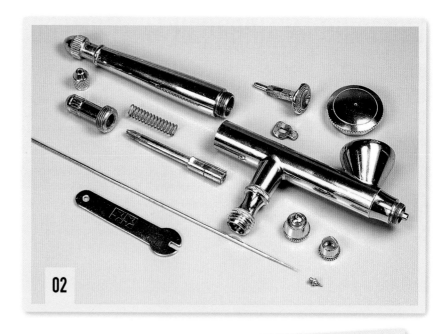

PHOTO 3:

I have two compressors that I use. The first in this photo was given to me while in Russia as a stop-gap prior to purchasing a better one. It is a rather low-end inexpensive type. The airflow is controlled by the small knob on the right hand side. This knob later had to be taped in place as the compressor's vibration during use would cause it to come loose slowly increasing the flow through my airbrush. Although basic and more for beginners, it does work and a few of the models in this book were painted only using this compressor.

PHOTO 4:

Silent compressors like this one are much more common amongst hobbyists. Models like these usually contain an airflow regulater, automatic on/off pressure switches and thermal overload protection. They also contain a moisture trap. Moisture traps keep condensation from accumulating in your air hose creating drops that will cause the airbrush to "spit" affecting the soundnes of the base coat.

If you take care of your compressor maintaining it regularly, these devices will most likely last you a lifetime. Now lets look at some common problems usualy encountered when your airbrush and compressor are not properly set.

TROUBLESHOOTING YOUR AIRBRUSH

WHEN AIRBRUSHING THERE ARE A COUPLE OF THINGS THAT YOU SHOULD KEEP IN MIND IN ORDER TO OBTAIN GOOD RESULTS.

You should be familiar with your airbrush. The kind of paint you are working with is also important because different types of paint will give various results. Even different brands of the same types of paint contain their own characteristics. The two major things that you will need to keep in mind are the air pressure and, most important, the paint-to-thinner ratio. All of these factors need to be considered for the various tasks that you will need an airbrush for. For a base coat it is always recommended to use a thin mixture. Most modellers prefer a mix of 30% paint to 70% thinner ratio. This ratio can vary depending on the paint. I airbrush some primers and varnishes at a 70% paint to 30% thinner ratio. When airbrushing scale models you should start with applying rather thin layers using quick passes when applying a base coat for example. Two or three thin coats will always lead to a more satisfying result than one thick coat. When creating camouflage stripes or blotches the paint to thinner ratio will sometimes vary depending on the result you would like to obtain. If you are after a rather hard edged pattern it is recommended to use mixture containing a bit more paint. Patterns with softer edges are best applied using a mixture with more thinner. Of course the air-pressure that your compressor is set to also has an effect. Again, understanding all of this will come with practice.

Before even getting your airbrush close to your model you should check the result first on a piece of scrap paper. The following pictures display typical unwanted results that you may encounter when airbrushing. The accompanying text will give you an idea on what needs to be changed to improve the outcome. Another source of problems is the condition of the airbrush. You need to make sure that it is always clean and that there are no paint residues from past projects inside adhered to the nozzle and needle.

 PHOTO 1:
The result seen on this first example indicates that the paint is clearly too thin. Extra paint needs to be added to the mixture.

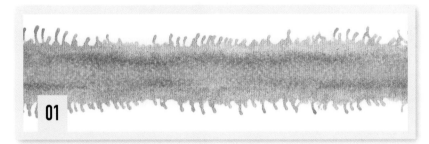

 PHOTO 2:
An uneven application with wildly dispersed speckles probably mean that this time the paint is too thick and more thinner should be added.

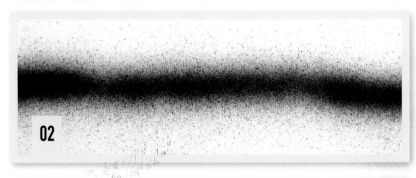

 PHOTO 3:
On this example two errors have occurred. First, the paint mixture is too thin containing not enough paint and the air pressure is set too high. The so called "spider legs" are always an indicator of excessive the air pressure.

 PHOTO 4:
If your application looks similar to this you might want to increase the air pressure of your compressor as it is a bit too low.

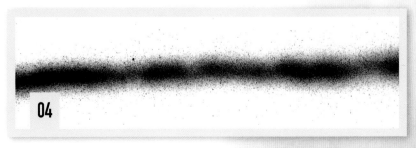

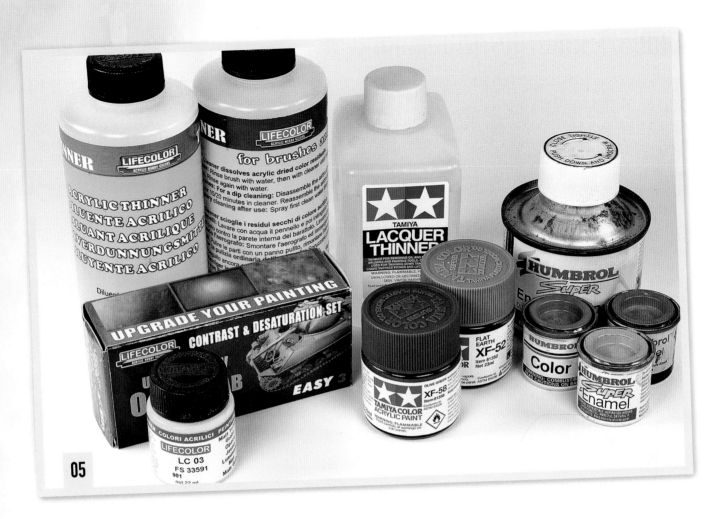

05

PHOTO 5:

Every brand of paint usually has their own thinner and/or airbrush cleaner. It is recommended to use such products together as they correspond to the chemistry of the paint. Horrible clogs can result in your airbrush otherwise. Make sure that your airbrush is completely cleaned after each session. This will save you a lot of stress the next time you are painting that model you recently spent so much time assembling.

06

PHOTO 6:

Finally, be responsible and wear a particle mask and have proper ventilation when airbrushing. Breathing in fumes ceased by the different thinners can result in long-term chronic health problems. I would recommend speaking to the people at your local hardware store to find one that best works for you. Let's now look at applying a basecoat.

AIRBRUSHING A BASECOAT

NOW I AM GOING TO DEMONSTRATE SOME TIPS TO HELP YOU APPLY A GOOD SOUND BASECOAT FREE OF FLAWS SUCH AS DUST.

We will begin with preparation of the model. It should be cleaned prior to having any paint applied. Securing small parts such as hatches and wheels in order to keep them from being blown across the bench by the airbrush is also handy. Sometimes the model contains metal parts that need to be primed. Then we will look at techniques for applying a smooth basecoat that evenly covers the model.

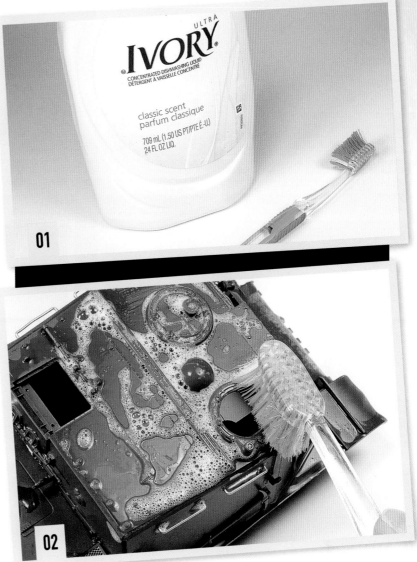

01

PHOTO 1 AND 2:

After assembly I would always recommend first cleaning your model with dish washing detergent using an old toothbrush in order to remove mould releasing agents, dust, oils from your fingers and liquid fluxes (if your model contains soldered PE parts) which might affect or be visible through the basecoat. If your model has a lot of fine PE parts I would use an old paint brush to clean those delicate areas. Please note that the soldered areas will oxidize developing a bit of texture after you wash the model so do not clean it until you are ready to apply the basecoat. Afterwards place the model onto a paper towel and let it dry overnight.

02

PHOTO 3 THROUGH 7:

The JSU, T-34 and Tiger I models are examples of some of the details and sub-assemblies that I keep separate when painting a model. Keeping these parts un-glued allows you to handle them for better positioning during the application of time-consuming effects such as chipping. Most of these parts can easily be held in place using Blu-Tak while airbrushing the basecoat. Make sure that you cover areas where parts are to later be glued using masking tape or liquid mask.

03

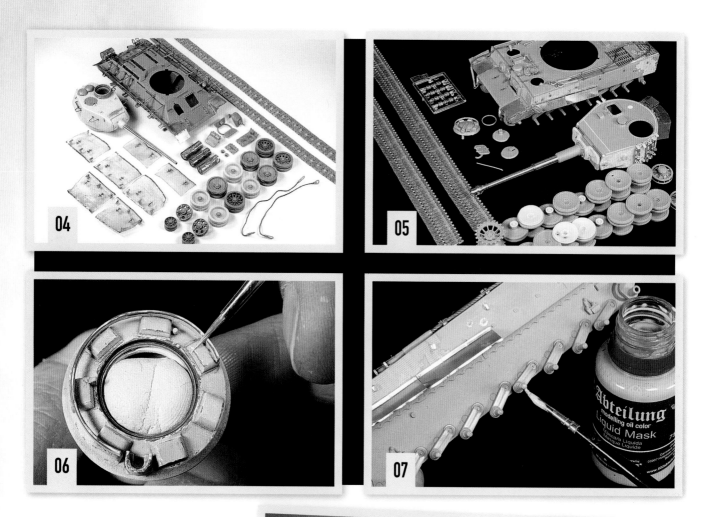

PHOTO 8:

» Let's use this E-50 as an example. Prior to airbrushing the basecoat I applied a few coats of primer over the larger photo-etched parts. You will find that most paints adhere well to the plastic of injection moulded kits. Priming the whole kit will just give you another layer of paint that might only help to hide fine details.

PHOTO 9 AND 10:

» I mixed a tone representing a light red oxide primer using Tamiya paints. I kept the tone light as I knew the weathering steps applied after would darken it to a realistic looking primer red. I blended the tone to about one-part paint and two parts Lacquer thinner. Tipping the cup back and forth and viewing how quickly the paint runs back down the side is a simple way for you to get an idea as to how much the paint is diluted. How much you choose to thin the paint to your personal liking will come with experience.

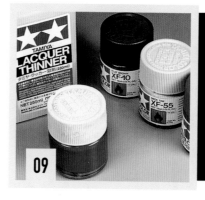

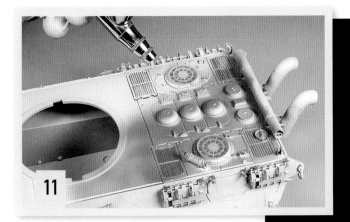

PHOTO 11 THROUGH 13:
I usably set the regulator on my air compressor to about 18 PSI when spraying a basecoat. You should always airbrush the replica from at least four or five different angles (front, back right, and left) to ensure that you have a good coat inside and around all of the details. As a result of this you will need to add numerous thin coats. It is important that your paint is properly diluted. Always keep your airbrush moving making passes with a circular motion evenly distributing the paint over the surface avoiding any buildup or puddles. I normally airbrush four to five even fine coats over the model.

PHOTO 14 THROUGH 16:
Tape and paper along with old paintbrushes are great for holding and positioning parts during airbrushing. Old unneeded items such as this resin accessory are also great for securing parts. The hatches were stuck to this accessory using Blu-Tak.

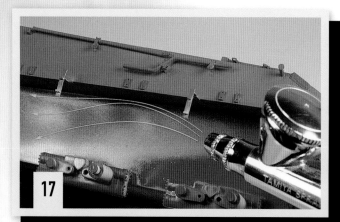

 PHOTO 17 THROUGH 19:
An important thing to keep in mind while applying a basecoat is the angle of your airbrush. As in photo 17, always keep the airbrush slanted and not perpendicular to the surface you are painting especially in corners. This will ensure that all of the overspray is blown away from the models surface. Pointing your airbrush directly toward the part as in photo 18 may result in overspray building up causing areas of fine texture. This texture can cause unwanted matt regions on satin and glossy finishes while also affecting some of the upcoming weathering steps such as washes for example.

 PHOTO 20 AND 21:
After obtaining a good smooth base coat over the entire model I will often brush different shades mixed form Lifecolor or Vallejo acrylics onto some of the different components for contrast. Modellers often refer to this as "Paneling". The black fenders on this example were also brush painted at this time.

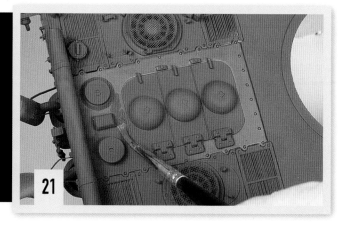

PHOTO 22 THROUGH 25:

These round vents are one example as to the advantage of temporarily attaching components by means of Blu-Tak instead of gluing them permanently. After airbrushing the basecoat I was able to remove this piece and quickly airbrush the light grey tone representing the zinc phosphate primer. A few coats of Vallejo matt were used to finish the flat base-coat insuring that the brush painted acrylics and primer red surfaces had an unified matt texture.

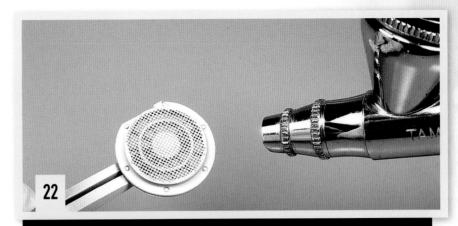

22

23

I strongly recommend that you always clean everything with dish washing detergent and warm water prior to airbrushing. Try to keep as many components and sub-assemblies removable from the model as possible. This will let you easily position the parts allowing for better results while also permitting you to save time during painting and weathering as you will see. You can also see that a basecoat can consist of a few steps aside from airbrushing such as brush painting details to get some contrast amongst parts. A few nice coats of matt varnish, in this case, also where applied. Let's now move on to airbrushing a camouflage and some things to remember while doing so.

24

25

AIRBRUSHING A CAMOUFLAGE

AIRBRUSHING CAMOUFLAGES HAS NEVER BEEN A STRENGTH OF MINE.

I sometimes feel a bit nervous when applying these types of patterns especially those applied in the field during World War Two. Being tense and a bit stiff can detract from the natural look often observed in photos. Here I will demonstrate a few methods that I have developed to help me obtain a more natural-looking field-applied camouflage.

As I said earlier you should be familiar with your airbrush and the paints you are working with. A double action airbrush should be used for these tasks. Tamiya paints diluted with lacquer thinner have always worked well for me when airbrushing a camouflage. Lifecolor diluted with their thinner is another and less toxic mix that I have had success with. Remember that different brands of paint have their own characteristics and you should find one that you are comfortable with. Also keep in mind the air pressure and paint-to-thinner ratio.

The camouflage we will apply to this T-34 will be done using Tamiya paints diluted with lacquer thinner. The mix used here was about 40% paint and 60% thinner. My air compressor was set at 18 to 20 PSI. Remember that this paint to thinner ratio and compressor settings could vary a bit depending on the equipment you are using.

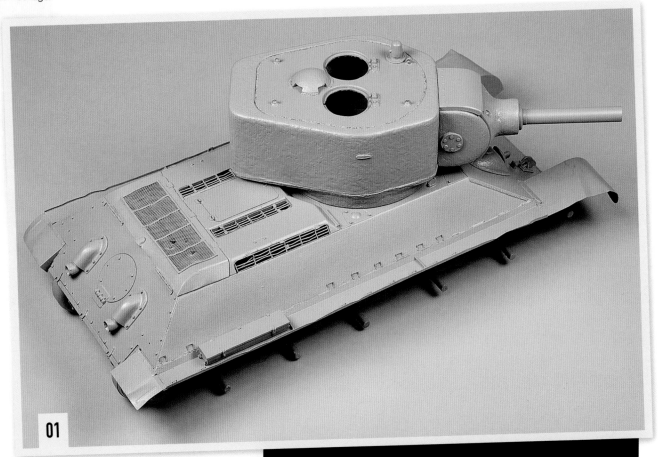

01

PHOTO 1 AND 2:

After practicing on a piece of paper I airbrushed an outline of the pattern over the model. The nozzle should be close the subject as seen in the photos in order to keep the edges of the lines tighter. You only want to gently pull back on the trigger of your double action airbrush spraying a very light stream while always keeping the brush in motion. If you find that you are unhappy with the pattern of the outline you can simply cover the unwanted parts with the base colour and then reapply them.

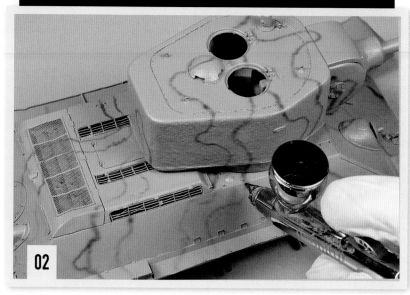

02

PHOTO 3 THROUGH 6: Once content with the pattern I carefully fill it in. After the camouflage I usually apply the markings then airbrush a few good coats of varnish over the model. The varnish will help to ensure that the tones used for the basecoat and those of the camouflage contain the same type of finish. In this case I added a satin finish that would be better for the anticipated washes in the upcoming steps.

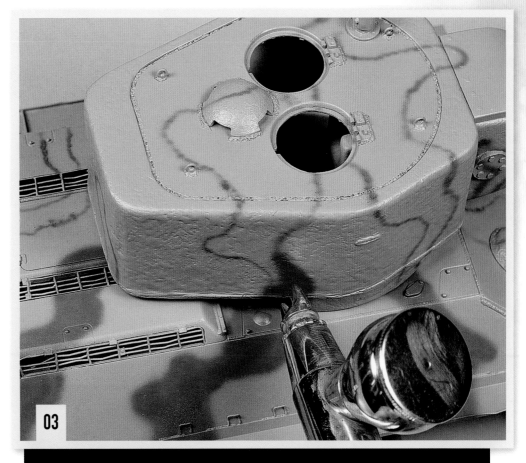

03

04

05

06

07

PHOTO 7:

As I mentioned, switching back and forth between colors when airbrushing a camouflage will allow you to tweak unwanted areas obtaining better results. The tight linear camouflage pattern on the 17cm cannon of this Geschuzwagen Tiger was obtained by applying the green camouflage over the basecoat. I went back over the areas of the pattern which I was unhappy with using the sand yellow basecoat.

PHOTO 8:

Switching back and forth between the colors of the basecoat and the tones of a camouflage in order to fix mistakes is not always an option. Much care had to be taken when applying the camouflage over this Panzer IV featuring Colour Modulation. The gradients in the basecoat would have made covering the unwanted areas of the camouflage very difficult reducing the natural shifting of the tones. We will cover applying camouflages over Colour Modulation later in this book.

How much you dilute your paint and what your compressor is set to plays an important role when airbrushing especially during spraying a camouflage. Practice your pattern first on an old model or piece of paper to make sure that everything is mixed and adjusted properly. Depending on the subject you may have the option of switching back and forth between the basecoat and the colour of the camouflage in order to obtain optimal results. After applying the basecoat and the camouflage you should clean the airbrush prior to putting it away. If you are familiar with your airbrush this should not be too difficult as I will show you next.

08

CLEANING THE AIRBRUSH

SO YOU JUST GOT YOUR BASECOAT AND CAMOUFLAGE FINISHED AND YOU ARE HAPPY WITH THE RESULTS.

It is now important that you devote a bit of time to disassemble and thoroughly clean the airbrush. One can quickly tell if any paint has built up inside of the nozzle of a double action airbrush by feeling if the trigger has become slightly loose when pulling back on it. If your trigger has any play it most likely means that your airbrush needs to be cleaned.

There are many different types of airbrush designs and some disassemble rather differently. This Tamiya superfine HG-SF model is a rather common choice amongst hobbyists. Let's use this as an example as the same cleaning steps will apply to most other type of airbrushes.

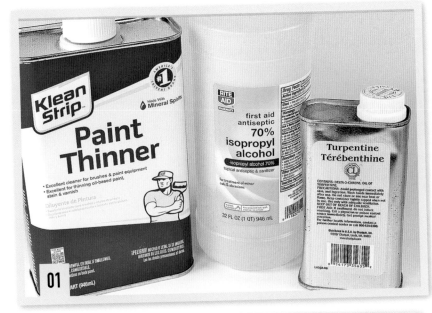

» **PHOTO 1:**
As already mentioned it is best to use the thinner or brush cleaner offered by the brand of paint you are using to clean your airbrush. Mixing different brands of paint and thinner together can cause the remaining paint inside of the nozzle to coagulate making miserable clogs that take much more time to clean. If you are knowledgeable of the brands you normally use, there are less expensive alternatives such as isopropyl alcohol or white spirits available in your local hardware, art and pharmaceutical stores.

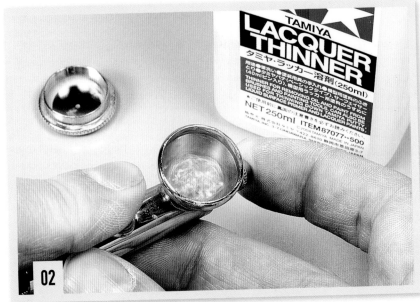

» **PHOTO 2:**
After applying the red oxide basecoat to my E50 I simply took the same lacquer thinner, used to thin the paint during the application of the base coat, to clean out the airbrush. I like to start by placing some of the thinner into the cup. Next I block the end of the nozzle while pulling the trigger forcing the air back up through the cup. The bubbles created will help to clean most of the paint away from the interior of the airbrush. After you can dump out the dirty thinner and/or spray it through the nozzle.

» **PHOTO 3 AND 4:**
Next unscrew the nozzle, slide the needle through the front and wipe it clean on a piece of tissue paper.

» **PHOTO 5:**
Over time there will usually be some of paint and dust collected inside of the nozzle. You can carefully scrape the inside of the nozzle and push the dry paint through the end using the needle. After simply place the disassembled airbrush down and let it dry overnight before assembling it again in the morning.

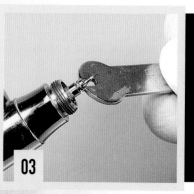

BRUSH PAINTING BASE COATS AND CAMOUFLAGES

AIRBRUSHING IS USUALLY THE PREFERRED MEANS BY MODELLERS FOR APPLYING COATS OF PAINT BUT THERE WILL BE CASES WHERE A PAINT BRUSH IS MORE SUITABLE.

Brush painting requires more time. More skill is also needed in order to avoid textures, like brush strokes, after the paint has dried that will affect the washes. If you are patient and thin the paint properly, brush painting large areas has its advantages.

In this example we are going to apply a hard-edge camouflage scheme. There are a number of methods for masking and airbrushing hard edge camouflages. Cut pieces of masking tape, liquid mask and even silly putty can be used. The problem is that these methods often require some touch up around the edges. Time is also needed to properly cut the pieces of tape to create intricate patterns. Liquid mask can be messy. Silly putty will break fine photo etched details. Painting a complex hard-edge camouflage by brush will give you more control while allowing you tighter edges between colors.

In this section I am going to now show you how I applied a complex hard-edged camouflage onto this JSU-152 using a paint brush. Unfortunately I only had one photo of the JSU-152 on which this replica was modeled. In this case I needed to study the camouflage in the photo carefully to get an idea as to how it might appear on the sides out of view in the photo.

> » PHOTO 1:
> After airbrushing a coat of green over the model using Lifecolor paints I drew the camouflage pattern using a pencil.

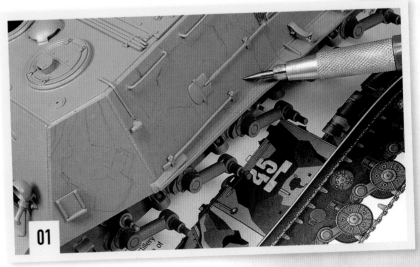

01

PHOTO 2 THROUGH 4:
I mixed the first tone from acrylics then added some water thinning the paint to the consistency of milk. Thinning the paints will result in a smoother finish with less brush strokes evident. I traced the outlines of the camouflage pattern using a new brush.

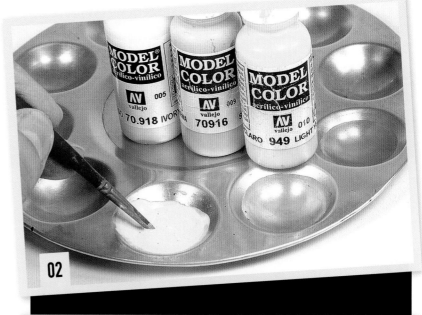

02

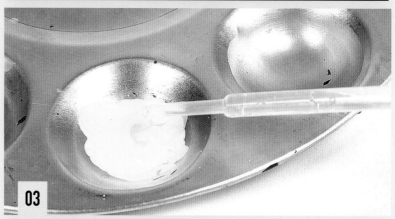

03

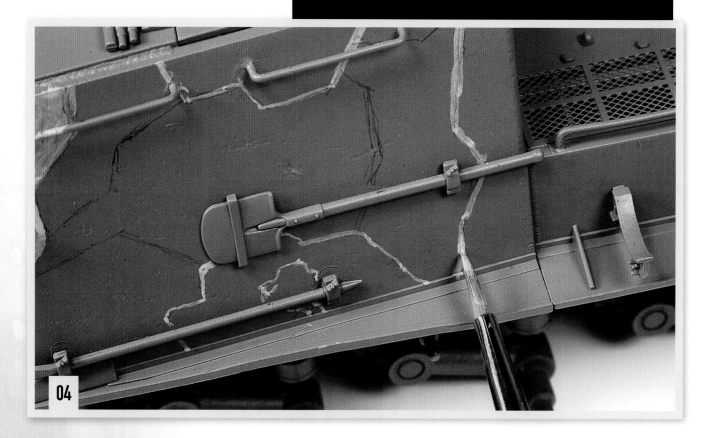

04

05

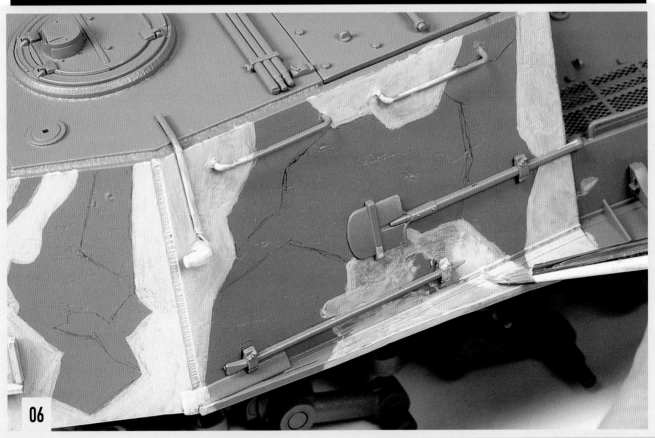

06

PHOTO 5 AND 6:

After tracing the pattern I painted the first coat of the tan areas making up the camouflage. Five to six of the thinned coats of the lighter sand colour were needed to get a good opaque tone over the darker green. When brush painting it is usually best to start with the lighter tones then move onto the darks. In the case of this replica, the actual vehicle contained a dark green basecoat. I opted to airbrush the green tone first finishing the upper hull, superstructure, chassis and wheels all at the same time. Choosing to paint the model in this manner resulted in me needing to apply more layers of sand over the darker green.

PHOTO 7 AND 8:

I moved onto the brown colour and finished with the black. When painting a camouflage in this manner always first mix plenty of each tone keeping them sealed in jars. Having each of the colors available will allow you to quickly paint back over areas where you made mistakes or are unhappy with the pattern. Once I went back and touched up a few areas I airbrushed the markings using stencils cut from paper. After I airbrushed a few coats of satin varnish over the entire model.

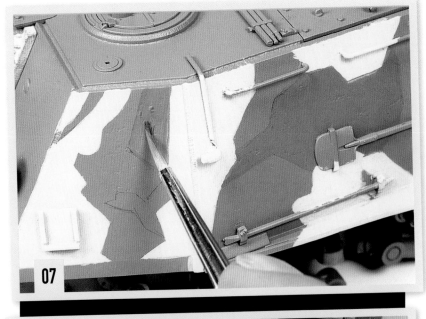

PHOTO 9 THROUGH 11:

It is best to finish all of the sides that you can distinguish in your reference photos first. After completing the visible parts it was easier for me to imagine what the patterns on the sides out of view might have looked like. The camouflage on the Tiger II was also painted by brush. I have seen many photos of this factory applied ambush camouflage pattern from all sides of these famous Tigers seen during the Ardennes offensive. To my dismay I was unable to find many images clearly showing the pattern on the upper hull and turret. Once I finished applying the camouflage onto each side referencing the photos, I was then able to design what might have been a fairly accurate pattern onto the tops of the hull and turret. In the case of the Tiger II I started with the light sand yellow tone than finished with the darker green and red-brown colors. Again it is usually better to start with the lighter tones depending on the subject. In the next part we will continue with base coat and camouflage application with the Colour Modulation Style.

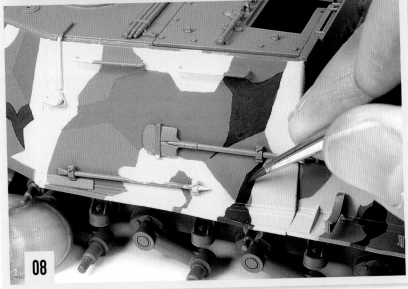

10

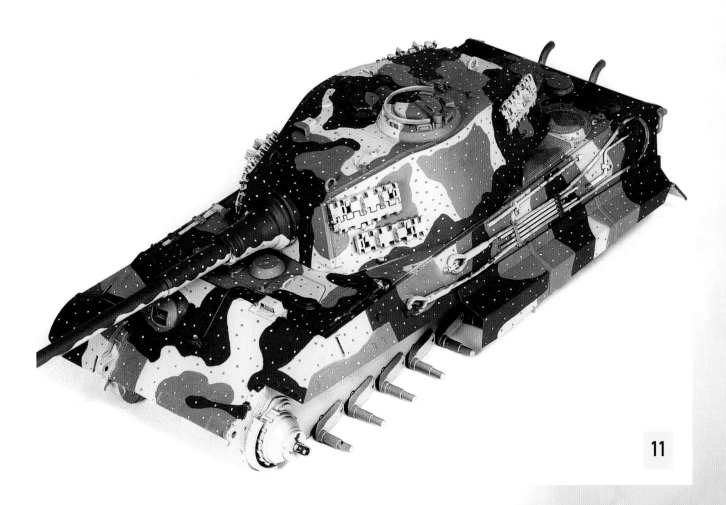

11

04 COLOUR MODULATION

COLOUR MODULATION IS A PAINTING STYLE THAT HAS EMERGED IN THE MODELLING WORLD OVER THE RECENT YEARS.

Colour modulation uses different light and dark tones throughout the various steps of the finish to accentuate volumes while also drawing attention to different details on a replica much like the classical artists did on their paintings during the 16th century.

I created this style in the evenings after work while in living in Spain. Modellers have been shifting tones and adding shadows in their base coats for years. English modeller Phil Stutcinskas was one of the modellers whom I observed shifting the tones upward with the base coats as seen on his famous Panzer IV that he took best of show with at Euromilitaire in 2007. With some advice from co-workers and other acquaintances in the modelling industry I experimented with what would become the colour modulation style for about three years while living and working in Northern Spain. My first attempt at colour modulation was this Krupp Steyr Waffen Trager. I found the finished modulation a little subtle. The KV-1 M42 was my second attempt to further modulate the colors this time shifting the tones towards the front driver's side of the vehicle. Positioning the light toward the front of this model also played an

important role in obtaining this photograph. This example easily demonstrates how colour modulation

gives the modeller another level of creativity with the model's finish.

Although the colour modulation again ended up a bit subtle for my taste, this Panther F was about my fifth attempt at experimenting with what would become this style. This paper panzer has been one of my most successful models to date. The Panzer IV later in this chapter was an effort to see how far I could exaggerate all of the tones starting with a dark brown colour and working up to almost a white. The extreme difference in tones on this example required me to also alter the colors during the rest of the steps needed to finish this model such as the washes, chipping effects and earth tones. Out of all of the models that I have finished the Panzer IV is probably my personal favorite.

On the LVT (A) I applied the colour modulation using more of the traditional artist rules of shading. I refer to this as the new Color Modulation Style. The Panzer IV and the LVT will also be covered later on in this chapter.

You will see throughout the rest of this book that the colour modulation style involves a number of techniques during the model's finish sometimes including the weathering steps depending on how much the modeller has decided to alter the tones when applying the base coat. This is why colour modulation is referred to as a style. In this chapter we will be looking at different examples and approaches to colour modulation. I will cover the traditional style of colour modulation along with a newer approach. We will begin with a typical example of colour modulation applied to a Tiger I.

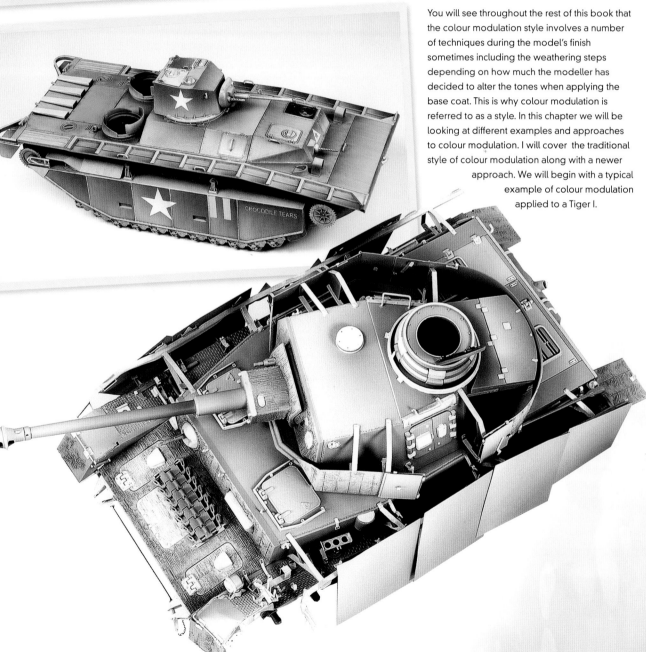

BASIC COLOUR MODULATION
FOR THIS FIRST EXAMPLE WE ARE GOING TO LOOK AT TECHNIQUES USED WHEN APPLYING A RATHER STANDARD EXAMPLE OF COLOUR MODULATION.

Here we will be simply shifting the tones of the base coat to break up the model accentuating the different parts and details of this Tiger I. Let's get started.

PHOTO 1 AND 2:

When using the colour modulation style I always start by adding a glossy black coat of acrylics over all of the areas that will contain shadows. I call this a shadow coat. Colour modulation requires you to build up layers of different tones when shifting from the darks to lights or vise-versa. The smooth glossy surface of this coat of black will help to reduce any texture that might develop as you continue to build up the layers of paint. Next I applied a dark yellow base coat using Tamiya acrylics onto the sides and upper parts of the hull and turret. This Tiger was going to have a winter camouflage so a few very small drops blue were added in order to help give a colder feeling to the finish. I placed this dark yellow mix into a spare jar.

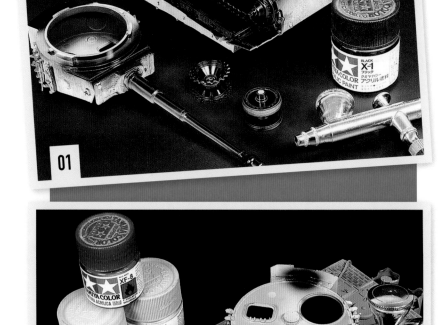

PHOTO 3 AND 4:

After adding a bit of gloss white to the dark yellow mix I masked off the fenders and started building up the lighter areas over the hull and turret. Next I removed the first lengths of tape, masked off the sides of the hull and started applying lighter tones onto the fenders creating horizontal gradients. Applying the gradients in this manner will help to distinguish each fender from the other. Remember that colour modulation is shifting tones to create contrast between parts and also stress volumes.

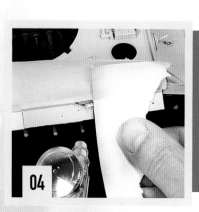

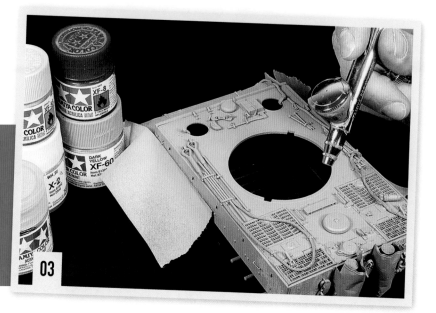

PHOTO 5 THROUGH 7:
After pouring a little of the dark yellow mix into another spare jar I added some more gloss white. I continued creating gradients on the upper hull adding the lights toward the outer edges working inward toward the darks creating a fake shadow around the turret. I masked and airbrushed some of the raised details using this lighter tone. Painting extruded details with lighter tones is a great way to make a model look more three dimensional. This BT-7A is a great example of using lighter tones to emphasize the raised details of a model.

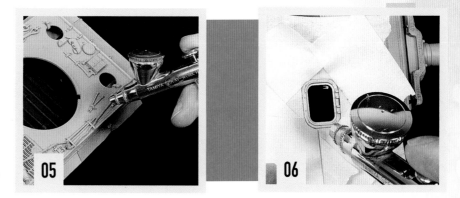

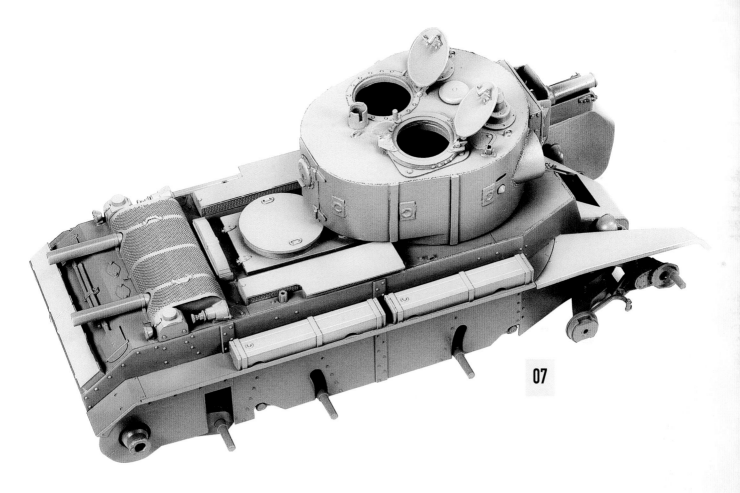

PHOTO 8 AND 9:
As I continued to lighten up the tones with white throughout the different steps, I added some yellow in order to give a little colour to some of these light grey highlights. Using these lighter tones I continued to mask off areas building up highlights over specific details. In photo nine I am airbrushing the light tone straight down over the top of the front hull plate, MG housing and the armoured enclosure over the drivers vision port. Note the subtle contrast created when applying the lighter tones over the fenders.

PHOTO 10 AND 11:
I masked the upper parts of the turret and highlighted them.

PHOTO 12 AND 13:
After the highlights I often go back over some of the shadowed areas with a darker shade of the basecoat. In this case I used a brown colour. I started by further stressing the shadows around the turret. I also used the brown to add more contrast between the hull and fenders. You can subtly create fine shadows with the aid of paper masks. Just airbrush the tone onto the paper at an angle that lets the overspray create a subtle shadow on the model.

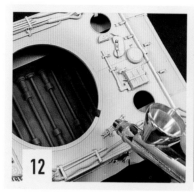

PHOTO 14 AND 15:
Photo 14 shows the Tiger I with the first step of colour modulation finished. It is easy to see how the various tones break up the different parts of the model. Note the three different tones subtly distinguishing the three plates making up the top of the turret. You can also see the brown tone on the upper hull around the turret creating contrast between these two parts. More yellow was added to some of the parts such as the hatches, middle fender on the side, mantlet and mid-section of the gun.

The wheels also exhibited tonal differences starting with the lighter outer ones and shifting to the darker ones on the inside. These wheels along with the undersides of the hull were the only areas where the earth tones needed to be altered when weathering this model.

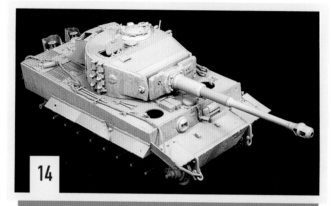

PHOTO 16 THROUGH 18:
Acrylic Lifecolor paints applied by brush were used to paint some of the smaller details that were more difficult to mask. Remember to thin the acrylic paints with water as discussed earlier to help make sure they brush on smoothly. Wipe the excess paint away on a piece of paper prior to painting the parts. You will need to apply two to three coats over the details depending on how much you thin the paints.

Smaller parts reflect less light than larger ones do. Therefore you can apply lighter tones to these finer details, such as the tool clamps, making them more noticeable after the weathering is completed.

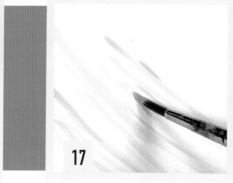
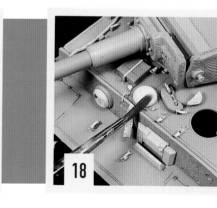

 PHOTO 19 THROUGH 22:
Next a light blue filter mixed from Tamiya clear was applied over the entire model to help give a cold feeling to what would be a winter Tiger I. This step would also help to add a bit of colour to the lighter, almost white details on the model. If your blue filter is too strong you will obtain more of a green tone as a result of the dark yellow base. More about filters will be discussed later.

These tonal variations will be less evident after the weathering but will help to subtly, in this example, create contrast between details while also emphasizing its volumes and details.

The VK3001 contains more of an exaggerated example of colour modulation. More attention was needed when applying paint chips and adding the earth tones over this model. Another exaggerated example of colour modulation will be used on the Panzer IV H in the next example. The shape of this model is also more complex then the Tiger I making it a fantastic subject for seeing just what can be achieved using this radical style.

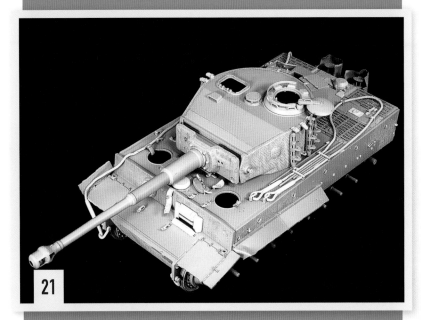

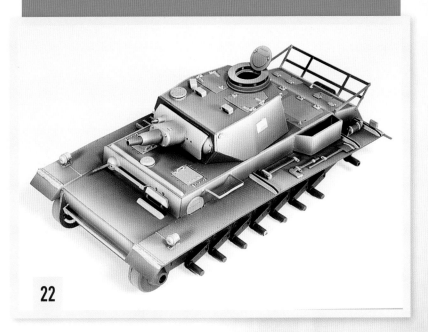

ADVANCED COLOUR MODULATION

IN THIS SECOND EXAMPLE OF COLOUR MODULATION WE ARE GOING TO FURTHER EXAGGERATE THE SHIFTING OF TONES ON THIS PANZER IV H.

The types of paints and techniques in this example are the same as explained earlier. Subjects like this Panzer IV containing details such as stand-off armour, or schürzen, allow you to get the most out of using the colour modulation style as I will now show you.

PHOTO 1:

I started with a shadow coat using Tamiya gloss black. I applied the black into the corners, on to all of the areas that would be behind the schürzen, beneath the turret and under the sponsons and hull.

PHOTO 2 AND 3:

Next I applied a brown tone over the sides of the hull and turret. I also airbrushed this tone onto the outer sides and upper inner areas of the schürzen. Note how I am starting to create upward gradients over the black areas on the sides of the hull. You can see that some of the gloss black is still evident on the sides of the turret behind the schürzen.

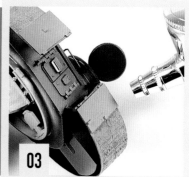

PHOTO 4 AND 5:

I poured some of the dark brown mix into another clean jar and added a bit of dark yellow. Using this lighter tone I continued creating gradients working upwards with the light tones over the brown colour applied before.

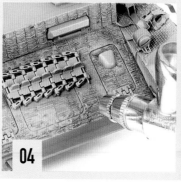

PHOTO 6 AND 7:

After adding a bit of gloss white to the mix I continued building up the highlights.

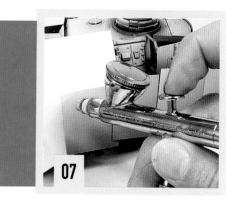

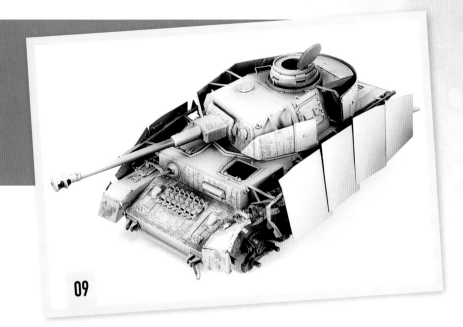

PHOTO 08 AND 09:

In photos eight and nine all of the gradients creating the shades and highlights have been airbrushed. Note the darker shadowed areas between the schürzen, lower hull beneath the fenders and around the commander's cupola. The lighter tones were airbrushed straight down onto the commander's cupola creating highlights on the upper edges. Note the different tones of the rear hatches on the upper hull. The gradients on the hull schürzen were applied diagonally to add further contrast amongst each other while still moving upward toward the highlights.

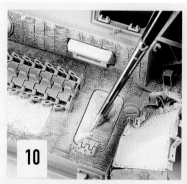

PHOTO 10 AND 11:

Like on the Tiger I brushed on lighter tones to some of the smaller raised details using a brush. Remember that you can add lighter tones to smaller details. Smaller details reflect less light and the effect will not be so evident on the completed model. Note how more of a yellow-brown tone was used on the details in the shaded areas beneath the turret and behind the schürzen.

PHOTO 12 AND 13:

Further contrast can be made amongst parts by blending oil paints. Subtle dry-brushing of light oils was also used to hilight the zimmerit surfaces.

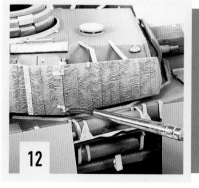

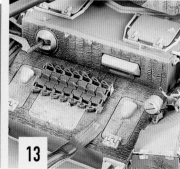

PHOTO 14 AND 15:

Photos 14 and 15 show the model with all of the different gradients and tones added. You can see where yellow was used to further distinguish the two top plates on the turret from each other while also adding a flare of colour to these grey-tan surfaces. Colour modulation is not just about lightning and darkening tones in order to add distinction amongst parts and create volumes. With this style you can also add more red, blue and yellow colors to shift the hues as another way to obtain contrast between parts.

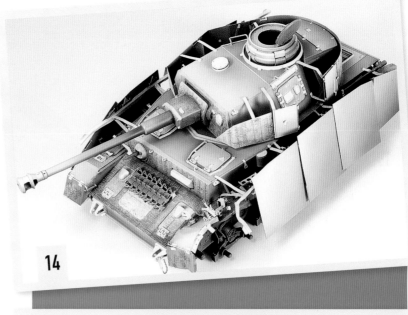

PHOTO 16 THROUGH 18:

Although five tones were mixed for the colour modulation in the base coat, I only needed a light and dark shade for each of the green and red-brown camouflage colors. The camouflage on this Panzer IV consisted of rather fine lines. Shifting the tones in these thin areas would not be too noticeable after weathering. First I airbrushed the complete camouflage using the light tones of each colour. Next I airbrushed the darker shades for the green and red-brown onto the lower parts and inside all of the shadowed areas.

PHOTO 19 THROUGH 22:
The final step needed before applying the decals was to airbrush the entire model with a few light coats of Tamiya clear. I mixed a light yellow filter for this step. This yellow tone added a bit of colour to the rather sand-grey highlights while subtly blending the different tones applied both with the airbrush and paintbrush. Note how more filters of the clear yellow were added to the second and forth hull schürzen to create subtle contrast from the first and third ones.

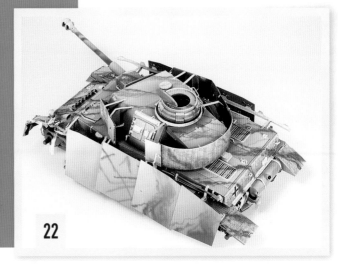

As wrote earlier, you can see how the lighter tones on the smaller details such as the hinges and braces for the schürzen mounts have been reduced after the weathering steps on the completed model. Note how the lighter areas and details such as the hatches, schürzen and cupola are especially evident making the model much more dramatic and three-dimensional in appearance. The biggest trick of all when using colour modulation is to know how to balance your application of the lights and darks effectively without making it look too obvious on the completed model.

You may need to also alter the tones of the chipping effects and weathering steps a bit when the colour modulation on a model is rather dramatic such as in this example. Although a bit time consuming altering the tones during these steps is rather easy. There will be some examples later in this book on doing so.

COLOUR MODULATION OVER CONTOURS

WE ARE GOING TO BE APPLYING THIS THIRD EXAMPLE OF COLOUR MODULATION ONTO A JS-3 TURRET CONTAINING CONVEX CONTOURS.

This time I will alter the tones to stress the dome-like turret of this JS-3. The types of paints and techniques in this example will be the same as explained earlier.

PHOTO 1 THROUGH 3:
I started this finish by applying a shadow coat onto the undersides of the hull and lower parts of the turret.

PHOTO 4 THROUGH 6:
Next I continued with a dark olive green and worked up toward the highlights. You can see that I am focusing the lighter shades of the gradients onto the upper parts of the radiuses. Yellow and white were used to lighten the shade. About five different green tones were used to create the various shades and gradients on this model.

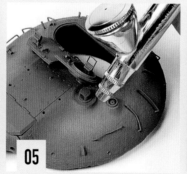

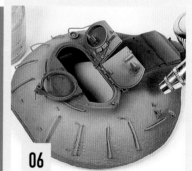

PHOTO 7 AND 8:
Sometimes a bit of imagination is needed as to where to place the highlights in order to get the most out of the colour modulation style. In this example highlights were added to the upper turret casting generating contrast between the mantlet along with the bolted plate on top. A different modeller might have instead decided to place the highlights onto the mantlet and/or top plate while also creating an equally effective result. Remember that this style contains a bit of flexibility.

PHOTO 9 AND 10:

Here is another quick example. Along with the typical vertical gradients on the walls I also added faint highlights over the corners and lower contours to help stress the shape of this T-34/85 turret. There are always different ways in which an individual can apply this style onto a model. That is why colour modulation gives us another level of creativity when finishing a model.

PHOTO 11 AND 12:

Once the highlights on the JS-3 turret were finished I went back over all of the corners with a darker olive green tone. You can see how the differences in tones stress the contours and edges on the turret.

PHOTO 13 THROUGH 15:

Again, acrylics were used to add further highlights to smaller details. The final step consisted of airbrushing a light green filter over the turret in order to subtly blend the different shades while adding a bit more colour to the highlights.

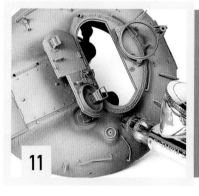

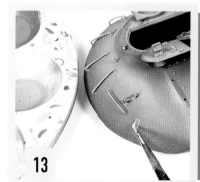

There are always different ways in which an individual can apply colour modulation onto a model. That is why the colour modulation style gives us another level of creativity when finishing a replica. To further demonstrate this lets move onto one more example of colour modulation reversing almost everything we have discussed in the three previous sections.

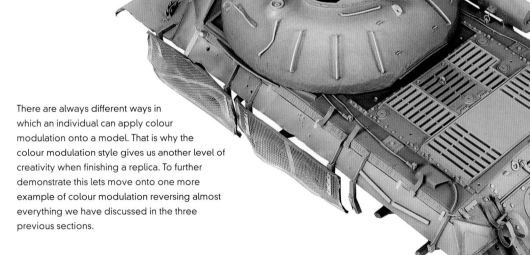

NEW COLOUR MODULATION

THERE ARE DIFFERENT WAYS IN WHICH AN INDIVIDUAL CAN APPLY THE COLOUR MODULATION STYLE ONTO A MODEL.

As you have now read this is why colour modulation gives the modeller another level of creativity when finishing a replica. To demonstrate this further let's now look at one more example of colour modulation reversing nearly everything we have looked at in the three earlier sections while still creating an equal or if not better looking result.

With this LVT I will be starting with the darks on the upper parts of the different surfaces and moving down toward the lights. This example will follow more of the traditional rules of lights and shadows taught in the basic sketching lessons that most of us remember during art class. In fact, I am finding this method to be more

of an effective approach when using the colour modulation style. Right now I simply refer to it as the New Colour Modulation Style. Although the application of the lights and darks will be reversed for this example we will be using the same paints and methods seen in the earlier three examples.

This LVT model has a rather complex shape. As a result a lot of masking would need to be applied and then removed throughout the different

application of the shades. Therefore I felt that it would be faster to mask and finish the colour gradients on one section at a time. I felt changing the paint in my airbrush for every shade in each section to be quicker then constantly applying and removing the tape as I worked through each shade. To do this I mixed five different tones starting from dark at number one up through the light at number five.

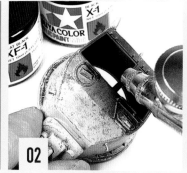

01   02   03

PHOTO 1 THROUGH 4:

The shadow coat was applied to the inner parts on the sides and beneath the hull. The inner areas around the openings of the hatches also got a coat of black. A light ivory tone was then applied to the interiors around the openings creating a subtle white gradient. This effect would give a nice shadowed look to the rather limited detailed visible interiors around the opened hatches.

04

05

06

PHOTO 5 AND 6:
Next I applied a dark grey coat to the outer sides and upper hull and turret.

PHOTO 7 AND 8:
I started by masking off and applying the full gradients onto the front and sides of the armoured housing protecting the driver and front MG operator. I also finished the area around the rear turrets that would mount the 30 caliber machineguns.

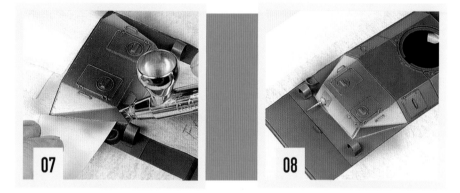

07

08

PHOTO 9 THROUGH 12:
Next I masked and applied each of the tones that would make up the gradients on the rest of the upper hull. I finished the sides then masked off and completed the top plates.

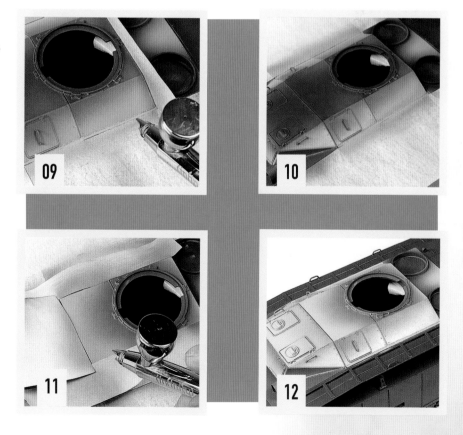

09

10

11

12

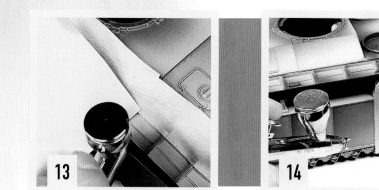
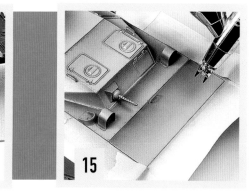

13

14

15

» **PHOTO 13 THROUGH 16:**
I masked and applied the gradients onto each of the fenders. Note that the gradients were applied with the lights starting at the inner corners moving diagonally outward to the darks creating contrast between each section. Contrast was created between the six large sections that make up each side of the lower hull in the same manner with the highlights terminating in the lower rear corners. The larger front plates were also masked them painted.

16

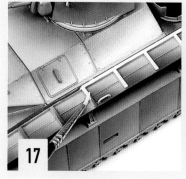

17

18

19

» **PHOTO 17 THROUGH 20:**
Different shades were painted over some of the details by brush adding more tones. In this case I focused the lights over the upper surfaces. During this time I had an afterthought to mix one more lighter tone and apply it to some specific details on the upper hull such as the hatches. Remember to continue adding more thinner to the lighter tones. A few light blue coats of Tamiya clear were airbrushed over the entire model to subtly combine the gradients and also prepare it for the upcoming weathering steps.

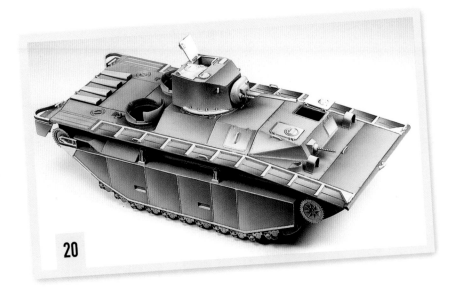

20

In this example you can see that I took an opposite approach when applying the gradients. As I said there are different ways in which an individual can apply this style onto a model. If done effectively it can really give a unique appearance to even the most common modelling subjects while drawing attention to details.

The LVT in this example, like the Panzer IV, has a rather large amount of contrast between the lights and darks. Some alteration of the colors in both the upcoming chipping and weathering effects would be needed between the light and dark areas. Methods on doing this will be discussed later on in this book.

Now we will move into the weathering steps. In the next section we will be discussing filters.

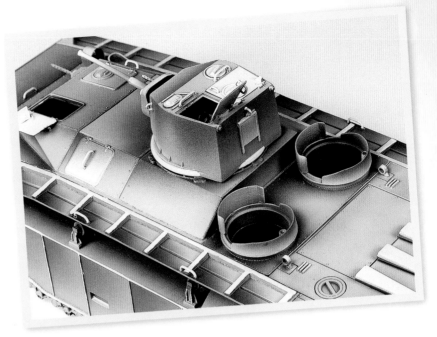

FILTERS

FILTERS HAVE BECOME SORT OF A FAD IN THE ARMOUR MODELLING WORLD.

A filter is a thin, almost transparent layer of paint, applied over a surface. Most of the time they are diluted to about 8 to 12 parts thinner and one part paint. This rather translucent layer can serve a number of purposes. Filters can be used to alter the tone and feeling of a base coat, subtly blend the colors of a camouflage or add different shades to a surface. Filters are sometimes confused with washes. Washes are also applied using layers of thinned paint but instead to create fake shadows around details and into seams helping to make these features more prominent. I will discuss washes in detail during the next chapter.

After the blue filter airbrushed back on page 34 I decided to apply another brown coat of clear adding a little more colour to this Tiger I practically over the lighter sand highlights and details.

Along with the tonal gradients of the basecoat, this LVT has different types of filters helping to make up the Colour Modulation. These filters are the different coloured clear varnishes and oil paints, helping to create contrast amongst the different parts and details.

Some examples for the different reasons to use filters are the following. Applying a transparent blue layer over a replica will give it a slightly colder looking appearance like the clear I airbrushed onto the Tiger I earlier in this book. Conversely a red filter will make a desert subject look warmer. If the green finish on your JS-3 looks rather dull a few filters of yellow will help to give more vibrancy to the tone. If the basecoat on that same JS-3 is too light a few Dark green, blue or brown filters will help to darken the tone a bit without subtracting too much from the vigour of the colour as demonstrated in the previous pages. You can also apply various coloured filters onto different surfaces of a model creating faint contrast between areas and parts. A matt varnish is also a type of filter. Applying fine specks of paint over a surface using a technique called Speckling is another type of filter. Fading with oil paints is another type of filter and will be demonstrated in the upcoming chapters.

You can create filters using most types of paints. There are also a number of products on the market. Today, probably due to a result of available products, filters are often applied using a paint brush. When applied with a brush filters work best over a matt surface as I will explain. As you have already seen Tamiya clear varnishes are also great for quickly applying filters. You can even use varnishes for adding contrast between different parts as I will now discus.

There are currently a number of products obtainable on the market to help you quickly apply filters. Today, probably due to a result of available products, filters are often applied by brush.

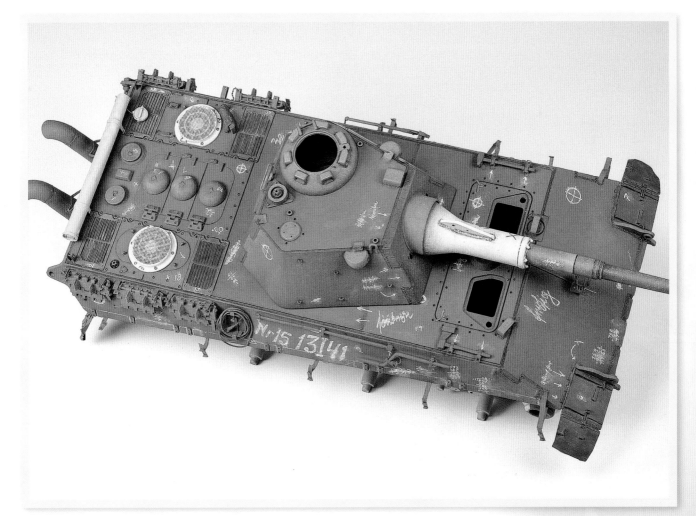

Applying fine specks of paint over a surface can also be considered as a filter. This technique is called Speckling and it was the primary method used in making the fabricator markings, which are actually white dry transfers, look as though they are made from dusty chalk.

AIRBRUSHING FILTERS

AIRBRUSHING VARNISHES AND CLEAR PAINTS ALLOW YOU TO APPLY FILTERS EVENLY OVER A SURFACE WHICH CAN OFTEN BE DIFFICULT TO DO USING A BRUSH.

 PHOTO 1 THROUGH 3:
For this example we will airbrush different clear tones onto the various sections of this grey LVT to work with the Colour Modulation creating additional contrast amongst the different parts.

01

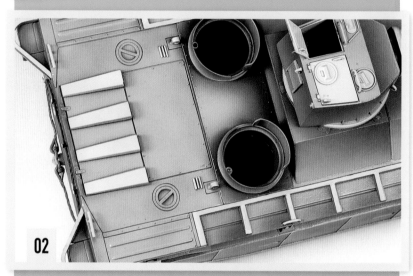

02

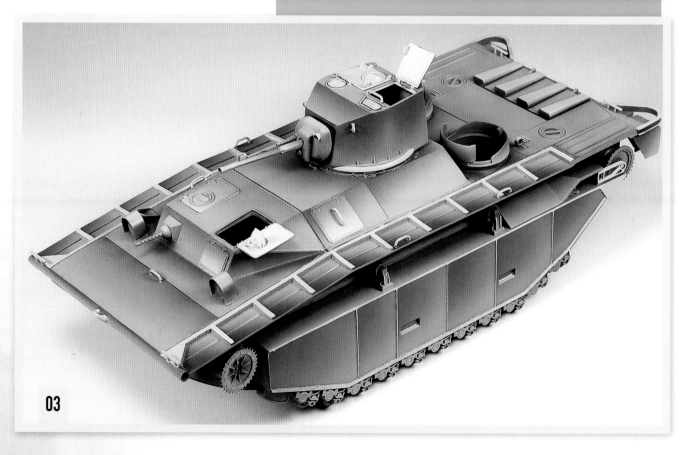

03

PHOTO 4 THROUGH 7:
I thinned some clear blue and airbrushed a few coats over some different masked panels to break up the model. Some modellers call this technique "Paneling". Masking tape and paper were used to keep any overspray free from the adjoining areas.

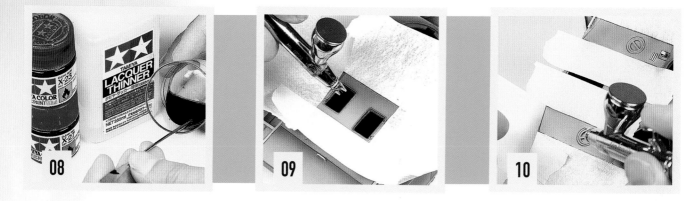

PHOTO 8 THROUGH 11:
For the sake of this example I took it a bit further and airbrushed a violet filter over a few more sections adding further contrast amongst the different parts of the model.

PHOTO 12 AND 13:
As shown earlier, the side skirts of this Panzer IV are another example of using airbrushed clear varnishes as filters to create tonal differences amongst parts. In this case clear yellow was airbrushed onto the mid and rear side skirts creating additional contrast amongst these four large pieces. The effect is less obvious but still evident on the weathered model.

13

PHOTO 14 AND 15:
A few coats of clear are sometimes all you need to help create contrast amongst parts as in the case of the panel on the upper hull of this T-72. The resulting glossy appearance of this detail is a bit more evident against the rest of the satin parts on the model. This is also a type of filter. Like in a photograph, details that are further from the lens always appear to be more matt in appearance. The matt coat applied over a model is also another type of filter. Next we will look at some examples of applying filters using a paintbrush.

15

14

APPLYING FILTERS BY BRUSH

PHOTO 1 THROUGH 4:

Now we will look at some examples of applying filters using a brush. In the first example I wanted to brush a few very faint dark blue filters over the surface of this winter Tiger to give it a colder damper feeling. I mixed a dark blue filter using artist oils and an enamel thinner. You might want to add less paint to the filter when brushing it over a satin surface. After wiping the excess away on a dinner napkin I brushed it over the surfaces of the model. If you are going to apply a filter by brush without first whipping the excess paint away you will only end up with more of a wash.

Filters applied using a paintbrush are a bit more subtle. They may also reduce the satin appearance of the model depending on the paint that you use. When brushing filters, three to four layers are sometimes needed to obtain your desired result. Make sure you give paints

04

like oils ample time to dry between each layer. The colour of the filter will become more evident as you build them up over each other. Applying filters with a paint brush does give you more

control over its distribution if you are only looking to apply it onto specific areas and details.

01

02

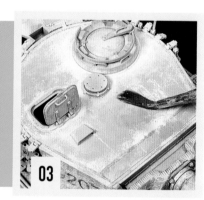

03

PHOTO 5 AND 6:

This E-50 has a matt finish. A matt coat of paint has a very fine coarse surface. The rough surface reflects light in many different directions. That is what makes a surface appear matt. Actual rust that you see on a piece of metal has a very coarse surface. This is why rust is always completely matt when it is dry. It is because of

this very fine rough surface that it is much easier to brush a filter evenly onto a matt surface. This fine rough surface will automatically absorb the

filter spreading it equally as you brush it over the model. The matt primer red surface of this E-50 will serve as a nice example.

05

06

PHOTO 7 THROUGH 10:

Remember to wipe the excess paint away onto piece of paper or napkin prior to brushing a filter. You can see in photo ten that the different coloured filters applied to the various surfaces of this E-50 helped to break up the different surfaces of the model.

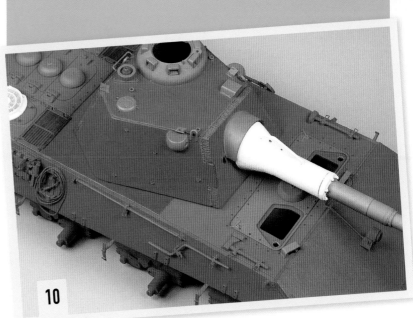

PHOTO 11:

Photo 11 shows an example of applying a maroon filter over a large surface to subtly blend a camouflage while adding a warmer hue to the overall finish. Again you can see in this example that a filter can be very faint as I brush it working from right to left.

Filters can be a very useful subtle technique. Further examples of filters will be used in conjunction with the various finishing steps discussed throughout the rest of this book. Before we end this chapter I would like to discus one more less common type of filter. Speckling faint semi-transparent muddled tones and textures over a surface will also help in this case to subtly unify colour modulation, while making white opaque dry-transfers look more like chalk.

SPECKLING FILTERS (CHALK MARKS)

SPECKLING PLAYS A MAJOR ROLE THROUGHOUT THE DIFFERENT WEATHERING PROCESSES THAT I APPLY TO MY WORK.

After a few years of relying more and more on this technique I decided to give it the name that I refer to it as now. I have published articles only about speckling highlighting the numerous possibilities of this technique for helping modellers to obtain natural finishes. You will see more examples of both when and where to use the speckling technique throughout the rest of this book.

Depending on how it is applied speckling can also be used as a filter. For this example we are going to apply some speckling along with other techniques to make the white opaque dry transfers on this E-50 look like worn powdery chalk marks. After studying reference photos I decided to produce with my company WILDER and use a set of dry transfers consisting of fine markings and other various German type

fabricator notes. These fine markings would have been very difficult to neatly write or paint to scale by hand. After applying the dry transfers I ended up using the speckling technique along with a few other steps to give these numerous small white transfers a look that resembled matt faded chalk. Here's how I did it.

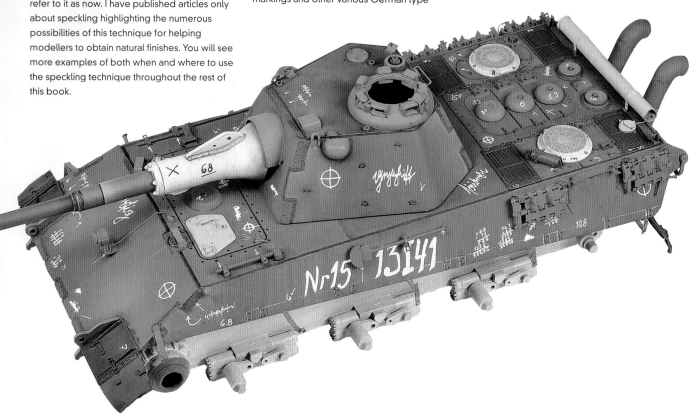

PHOTO 1:

You can use all types of paints when applying speckling effects. For this example I mixed a colour that matched the general tone of the E-50 using oil paints and pigments. The red pigments help to thicken the red oil paint while altering the colour to more of an oxide tone. You will also need to find a brush with stiff bristles. I modified the brush that I used throughout this book for speckling by cutting the bristles down to about half the original size.

PHOTO 2:

Like with most techniques, the more paint thinner that you add to a mix when speckling, the less opaque the effect will be. After quickly dipping the edge of my modified brush into the pool of enamel thinner I mixed some of the oil paint with the pigments on the pallet as shown.

PHOTO 3 THROUGH 5:

Sometimes it is a bit difficult to regulate the mix of mediums when using the speckling technique. Again, the amount of thinner added will affect its opacity. After wiping the excess paint away on a paper towel always first practice on a clean surface to make sure that the specks will be deposited to your liking. I wanted the first layer to consist of larger more transparent spots. Once content with the appearance during testing I speckled it onto the model. Masking is usually needed to keep unwanted specs of paint from getting over the different parts of the model. Always have plenty of masking tape and paper nearby. This model was rather easy because most of the surfaces had the same primer red finish.

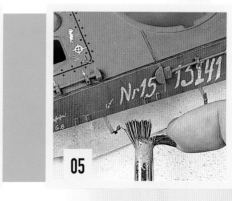

PHOTO 6 THROUGH 9:
Less thinner was added in order to keep the second coat of speckling more opaque. The advantage of using oils and enamels when speckling is that they dry slowly allowing you to blend and wipe the effect away using enamel thinner. These areas that you might want to clean for example are where the speckling may have been applied too heavily or on parts that you would prefer to not have this effect present such as windshields. Because of the amount of oil paints used, I needed to let the model sit for a little over two days before I could continue.

PHOTO 10 THROUGH 12:
I decided to apply a few more steps to further enhance the chalk marks. Small areas of White Lifecolor acrylics were randomly applied over the transfers using a fine brush to create less worn areas while giving a more random faded appearance to the markings. White pigments added a bit of a dusty look further emphasizing the appearance of chalk.

13

14

PHOTO 13 THROUGH 14:
You can see in photo 14 how the two layers of speckling effects gave the dry transfers more of a worn semi-transparent chalky appearance when comparing it to photo 13. It is important to also note that speckling applied heavily in this manner will reduce the contrast amongst parts achieved previously by the different gradients and filters used to help create the subtle Colour Modulation.

PHOTO 15:
This strip once more shows the two different transparent speckling steps used. These two semi-transparent coats work more like filters making the transfers appear to be faded and worn.

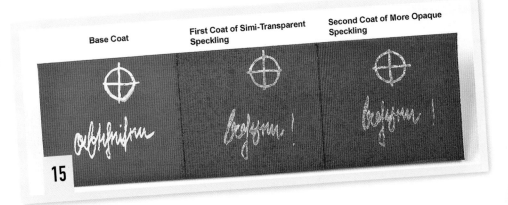

| Base Coat | First Coat of Simi-Transparent Speckling | Second Coat of More Opaque Speckling |

15

PHOTO 16:
The photo of this sand yellow Panther F schmalturm shows another example of applying speckling lighter amounts of paint to enhance chipping effects. Although similar to what I just demonstrated above I would not consider this a filter due to the much lighter amounts of paint being applied. I will discuss some more examples like this later.

I would like to point out one more thing about chalk marks prior to moving on. The worn appearance of the large chalk markings on the superstructure of this Ferdinand were obtained using a method referred to as the hairspray technique. We will be using the hairspray technique in a number of examples thoughtout the rest of this book. You will discover that there are usually different ways to get desired results. The markings on this superstructure were painted by hand making the hairspray technique possible. As a result of the dry-transfers used on the E-50 I needed to resort to speckling in order to obtain the same finish.

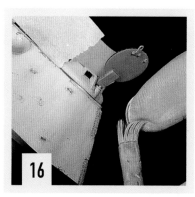

16

06 APPLYING MARKINGS & INSIGNIA

IN THIS SECTION I WILL COVER SOME METHODS FOR APPLYING MARKINGS.

Numbers and insignia play a very important role in creating an interesting replica of any type. In fact I sometimes choose the subjects that I want to build based only on the type of markings that they carry. Numbers, insignia and other types of markings should be authentic looking. They should be sharp and clean when necessary or appear to have been hastily applied as is sometimes the case. Normally the best time to apply markings is right after the basecoat

camouflage and filters prior to washes. Some modellers like to apply the markings after the washes so that they do not get discolored by the effect. I usually prefer applying them prior to washes. Washes are the first weathering step in my opinion, and the markings should usually be weathered with the rest of the basecoat but this decision is up to you. When to apply markings also depends upon the subject.

There are a number of methods and products available to modellers for applying realistic looking markings. Some of these methods and products require a bit of practice in order to properly apply them. Occasionally we are lucky,

sometimes markings on the actual vehicles influencing our models were hastily applied by the crews. This is common with WWII Soviet armour subjects for example. In this case you can simply paint the numbers and insignia by hand.

Accurately painting markings using a paint brush will naturally give you the best results. The problem with this is that much of the time markings are rather detailed and neatly applied. In this case one will usually need to resort to decals, dry-transfers, stencils and/or masks. All of these methods will be discussed in this chapter. Let's start with an example on using decals.

APPLYING DECALS

DECALS ARE ONE OF THE MOST COMMON METHODS USED BY MODELLERS FOR APPLYING MARKINGS.

Decal sheets have always been included inside most types of scale modelling kits. The quality of decals can vary depending on the manufacturer of the kit. Decals included with some of the older low-end kits would be rather thick and quite evident on the completed model. Today most kits on the market include decal sheets of rather good quality. There are even a few after-market companies that specialize in only decals. I have had good results with most of them. You can also purchase blank decal sheets to design and print your own markings using graphic design programs such as CorelDRAW.

Most of the time you will only need to apply decals over a flat surface. Unfortunately there are sometimes rivets, panel lines and other small details located where the decal needs to be placed. Therefore you will want a decal setting fluid along with some patience in order to get the marking to properly lay flat over the details.

In this example we will be applying decals over a rough zimmerit surface. If one can properly get a decal to lie onto a coarse exterior such as this then simply laying a decal onto a flat surface will be rather easy. Let's get started using this Panzer IV turret as an example.

>> **PHOTO 1:**
The decals that I am going to apply in this example are offered from Echelon fine Decals. After market companies such as this offer a wide range of decal sheets usually focusing on specific subjects, theaters and/or campaigns.

>> **PHOTO 2:**
First cut the decal from the sheet as close as you can to the marking as possible. You will need to place the marking in water letting it soak for about a minute or two. It is usually best to use a decal set and there are a few on the market. I have always had good results using Solvaset.

PHOTO 3 THROUGH 6:

Apply some water onto the area where the decal is to be applied. Once its has had a bit of time to soak very carefully remove it from the backing and place it onto the dampened area.

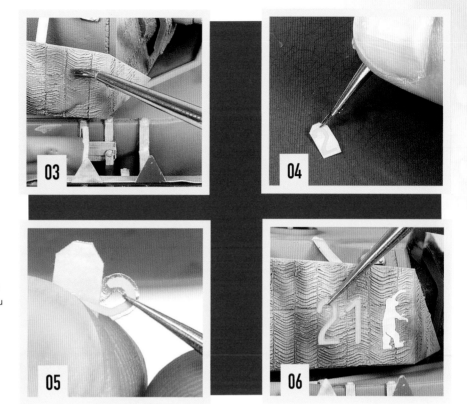

PHOTO 7:

Use the damp surface to slide the decals into their proper location. This process will be easier if the surface contains a satin or glossy finish. Once you have properly located the decals let them dry for about ten minutes. You can also carefully remove some of the excess water using a dry paint brush if you want to speed up the process.

PHOTO 8 AND 9:

After the decals have had about ten minutes to dry apply some Solvaset over them using a brush. The Solvaset will soften the decals letting them form and sink into the various contours of the rough surface. In this case the surface is very uneven and I would recommend putting the model down and letting the decals set overnight.

After waiting for 15 to 24 hours I found air pockets between the dried decals and some of the recessed areas of zimmerit. To fix this problem I used a new sharp hobby knife to lightly puncture some fine holes over the air pockets, applied some more Solvaset, and let the model set again for another six or seven hours. You might need to repeat this process a few times (I needed at least four times for this example) until the decals are laying completely flat on the rough surface.

10

11

 PHOTO 10 THROUGH 12:
After the decal was lying completely flat I airbrushed the entire model with a coat of gloss using Tamiya clear paints. The clear will help blend the glossy surface of the decals with the rest of the finish on the model reducing a mistake commonly referred to as silvering. Silvering is when the surface of the decal has a glossier (or different) finish then the rest of the model making the clear film around it obvious and the marking unrealistic.

12

13

PHOTO 13 THROUGH 16:
In the case of this unique T-55 engineering vehicle modeled by renowned Finish Modeller Jari Hemilä custom decals needed to be made. After designing the markings in CorelDRAW they were printed onto a blank decal sheet. In this example an enamel satin coat was applied over the decals to seal and protect them from the decal setting solution prior to cutting and locating them onto the model using the methods seen in the previous example.

Good decals are great if your model contains many complex markings and insignia. An alternative to decals are dry-transfers. Let's now look at a quick example about how to apply them.

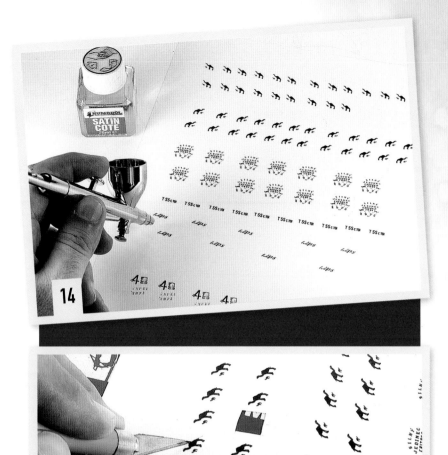

DRY TRANSFERS

DRY TRANSFERS BECAME MORE ACCEPTED WITH ARMOUR MODELLERS DURING THE 90S BECAUSE THEY WERE AN ALTERNATIVE TO DECALS.

Dry transfers are much like those Presto Magic sets that were popular during the seventies and eighties. Like decals they come on sheets.

 PHOTO 1 AND 2:

To apply dry transfers you will first need to peel away a protective film on the back side. Next you will want to cut the markings from the plastic film then locate it onto the model. Use tape to aid in firmly keeping the transfers in place.

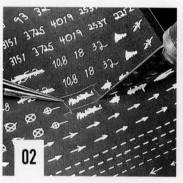

 PHOTO 3 AND 4:

Use a blunt object to rub the back side of the plastic backing forcing the transfer to stick onto the surface of the model. It is very important that the backing is firmly attached to the surface. If it moves at all while you are rubbing it the marking underneath will tear. After rubbing, carefully lift away the plastic backing leaving the marking attached to the surface.

I found that you need to push harder when applying certain transfers than with others. If you are using a good set of transfers the plastic backing will sometimes start to lift away from the markings as you try to tape it onto the surface. Normally I will apply a matt, satin or gloss coat over the model after the transfers are applied.

As I mentioned, with some brands the markings will come free more easily from the plastic sheet than with others. Many times I have pulled the

plastic film away after rubbing a marking in place and to my dismay found parts of the transfer still attached to the sheet. During these frustrating moments you will need to relocate the sheet getting the bits back in place and rub them some more.

Today dry transfers are still fairly popular with a number of companies offering their own ranges. You can usually find dry transfer sheets to fit much of your needs ranging from most types of markings, flags, instrument dials and even 3-D rivets and weld seams.

If the markings on your replica are rather simple it may just be easiest to paint them on using a fine brush or stencil. Applying numbers and insignia with these methods will most likely give you the best results. Let's now look at a few techniques often needed when painting markings buy hand.

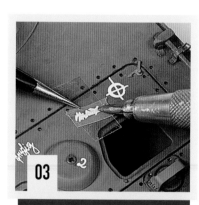
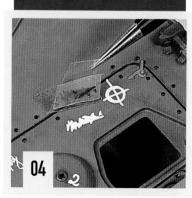

PAINTING MARKINGS BY HAND

OBVIOUSLY IT IS BEST TO APPLY SIMPLE MARKINGS USING A PAINT BRUSH OR STENCILS WHEN POSSIBLE FOR THE MOST AUTHENTIC LOOKING RESULTS

We will discuss stencils in the next segment. When painting markings by hand you will not encounter problems such as silvering that you sometimes see with poorly applied or low-quality decals for example. Although my preferred method, painting markings free-hand using a brush has always been a weak area for me because I simply lack practice. I have learned through experience that you just need to relax and be confident.

A new hi-quality paint brush is most important. The Winsor & Newton Series Seven brushes are what I feel the most comfortable with when painting markings. I would also recommend enamel paints because they dry slower allowing you to fix mistakes. After about a day enamel paints should solidify fairly well. You should be able to apply enamel washes and other effects in controlled amounts over them without smudging or lifting parts of the paint away.

You need to plan carefully when painting large slogans by brush. You should know where the slogan will both start and end. None of the slogans on my Hetzer seen on page 64 were painted from left to right. Instead I started with the center letters of each word and then worked my way out to each end. Masking tape can aid you in this process. Let's look at a few examples.

01

PHOTO 1:
The sentences on the side of this Geschuzwagen Tiger Fur 17cm were a bit easier to apply because I was not too concerned as to where they would end. In this case off-centered hastily applied looking text would only add the authenticity of the part because these phrases were supposedly painted in the field by hand. I did want to keep the text fairly straight on the side of this tall vehicle.

PHOTO 2 AND 3:
Before starting I thinned the Humbrol paint using enamel thinner. A piece of tape was used to establish where the phrase would be while also working as a guide helping me to keep the letters in line with one another.

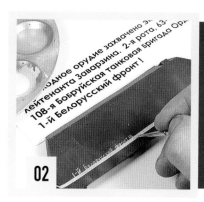

02

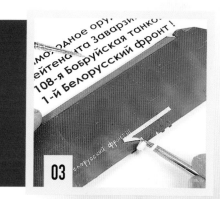

03

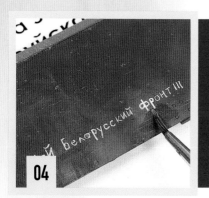

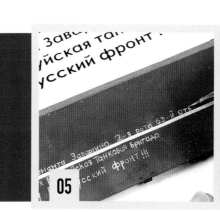

PHOTO 4 THROUGH 7:

In this case the surface of the model was completely matt. It is much more difficult to remove paints from these types of finishes even when it is still wet. I applied some touch-up around areas of the text where I ran into difficulties using the left over primer red Tamiya paint that I mixed in order to airbrush the model. Weathering will also help to subtly hide the areas on the text where faint smudges of white were left over from blending and removing mistakes.

PHOTO 8:

The thicker identification stripes and numbers on this JS-3 were painted like the camouflage on the JSU-152 earlier. I painted the outlines of the markings first then filled them in. Runs add much character and authenticity to hastily applied markings such as these. You need to be careful because it is very easy to paint runs like this that are too big and out of scale. Again I would recommend a new Winsor & Newton series seven brush for these details.

PHOTO 9 AND 10:
I waited until after the markings were finished in order to apply a few coats of Tamiya clear over the model. Applying the clear after ensured that both the markings and base green contained the same satin finish.

I try to apply markings by hand whenever possible. It is important to remember that when applying large markings or slogans you will need to know where they will both start and finish on the model. Whenever possible I also try to use stencils. Like brush painting, airbrushing with stencils can also help to give you very genuine looking markings. Let's look at a quick example.

I started with painting the center letters of each word on this Hetzer to help make sure that the slogans would be in the proper locations.

APPLYING MARKINGS USING STENCILS AND MASKS

LIKE BRUSH PAINTING I ALSO TRY TO USE STENCILS AND MASKS WHENEVER POSSIBLE WHEN APPLYING MARKINGS AND INSIGNIA.

Stencils or masks are also sometimes included with kits. Like decals and dry-transfers there are a number of aftermarket companies who offer stencils for everything from markings to entire camouflages. Edward from the Czech Republic offers a large variety of die-cut adhesive shapes that work rather well. Some companies such as MXpression from Germany even offer custom adhesive masks at customer request. Stencils are also available in photo-etch frets although these are difficult to use if the surface contains contours or details, as most often do.

01

PHOTO 2 AND 3:
You can simply make your own stencils and masks such as I did with this JSU-152. Make sure that you mask as much of the model as you can around the stencil or faint lines of overspray will be evident after it is removed. It is also important that you airbrush the stencil using light quick passes with your airbrush letting each coat dry before applying the next. Apply too much paint at once and it will be absorbed by capillary action between the mask and model creating an unwanted messy result.

02

03

PHOTO 4 THROUGH 6:
As with decals and dry-transfers you can paint over the markings after you remove the stencils creating realistic brush strokes on numbers and insignia supposedly painted in the field. Again I would recommend adding a satin or gloss varnish over the model once the markings are complete.

04

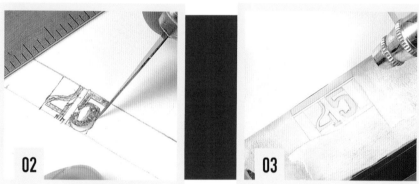

05

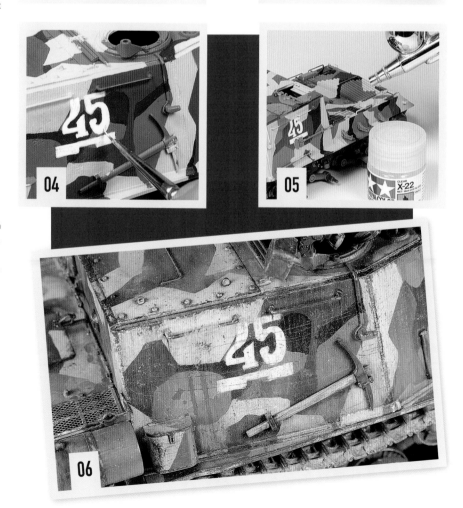

06

PHOTO 7 THROUGH 10:

I decided to order custom adhesive stencils from MXpression in order to create the markings on this LVT - (A) 1. One of the stencils which read, "Crocodile Tears" was a bit tricky to apply. After carefully removing the stencil some of the inner parts of the letters remained stuck to the backing. These fine pieces needed to be removed from the backing and properly located one at a time. This could not have been accomplished without a fine pair of tweezers and a new clean knife.

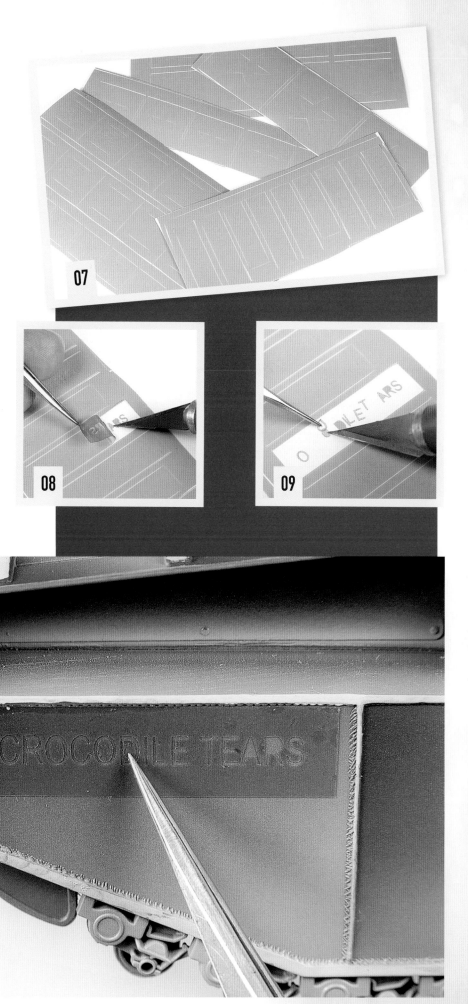

07

08

09

10

11

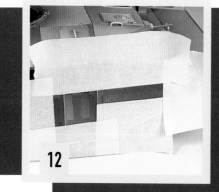

12

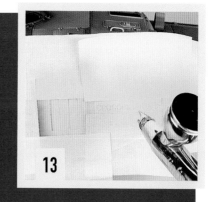

13

PHOTO 11 THROUGH 15:
I started with the masks only for the yellow insignia. After locating all of these markings I used a combination of masking tape and liquid mask to cover the areas and details around the masks. This would ensure that no overspray would be evident after the markings were airbrushed and the stencils removed. Remember to airbrush the stencil using light quick passes with your airbrush letting each coat dry before applying the next. Applying too much paint at once will allow it to be absorbed by the corollary action between the tape and the model.

I made the mistake of not giving the paint enough time to dry prior to removing the "Crocodile Tears" stencil. These areas needed to be carefully touched up using a fine paintbrush.

14

15

PHOTO 16 THROUGH 19:

After the markings had an hour or so to dry I applied the rest of the masks and airbrushed the white stars and numbers. I lightly rubbed the dry markings using very fine sandpaper to remove any edges created by the masks. This will give the markings more of a natural appearance. A coat of Tamiya clear was applied over the entire model after all of the markings where applied.

Appling realistic looking numbers and insignia is very important when creating authentic replicas of any type. This chapter demonstrated that there are a number of methods and products available to help effectively apply markings. Try to resort to using a paint-brush, stencils and masks when possible in order to get the best results. Decals are also fine if they are of good quality and you have an effective decal set.

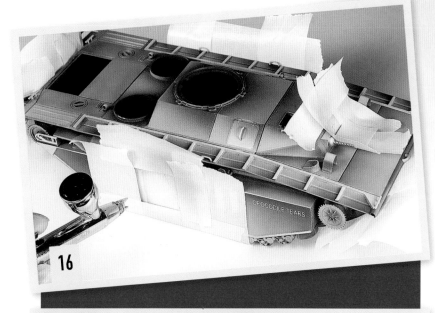

07 APPLYING A WINTER WHITE WASH

WINTER WASHES HAVE ALWAYS BEEN POPULAR AMONGST ARMOUR MODELLERS FOR A NUMBER OF REASONS.

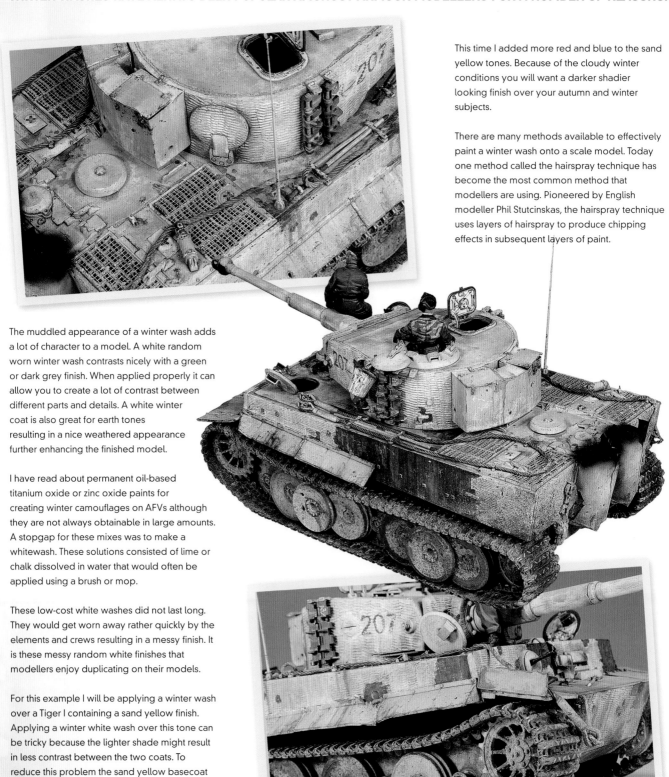

This time I added more red and blue to the sand yellow tones. Because of the cloudy winter conditions you will want a darker shadier looking finish over your autumn and winter subjects.

There are many methods available to effectively paint a winter wash onto a scale model. Today one method called the hairspray technique has become the most common method that modellers are using. Pioneered by English modeller Phil Stutcinskas, the hairspray technique uses layers of hairspray to produce chipping effects in subsequent layers of paint.

The muddled appearance of a winter wash adds a lot of character to a model. A white random worn winter wash contrasts nicely with a green or dark grey finish. When applied properly it can allow you to create a lot of contrast between different parts and details. A white winter coat is also great for earth tones resulting in a nice weathered appearance further enhancing the finished model.

I have read about permanent oil-based titanium oxide or zinc oxide paints for creating winter camouflages on AFVs although they are not always obtainable in large amounts. A stopgap for these mixes was to make a whitewash. These solutions consisted of lime or chalk dissolved in water that would often be applied using a brush or mop.

These low-cost white washes did not last long. They would get worn away rather quickly by the elements and crews resulting in a messy finish. It is these messy random white finishes that modellers enjoy duplicating on their models.

For this example I will be applying a winter wash over a Tiger I containing a sand yellow finish. Applying a winter white wash over this tone can be tricky because the lighter shade might result in less contrast between the two coats. To reduce this problem the sand yellow basecoat that I applied to this Tiger was darker than what I usually airbrush onto German armour subjects.

PHOTO 1 AND 2:

You can apply the hairspray straight from the can as many modellers do. I like to spray the hairspray into a cup then load it into my airbrush. Airbrushing the hairspray gives you better control of its distribution and the amount that you apply. If you apply too little the technique might not work. Apply too much and the succeeding layers of paint will crack after you wet and add the chipping effects to them. I have found that airbrushing three good coats often works fairly well. I would recommend trying this method on a few pieces of scrap plastic prior to applying it to your model.

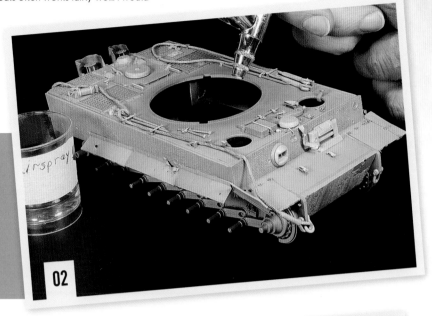

PHOTO 3 THROUGH 5:

One of the best mediums that modellers have had success with when using the hairspray technique are Tamiya matt paints diluted with water. In this case I thinned some Tamiya matt white paint to about one part paint and one part water and applied it in random amounts using my airbrush. A very small amount of blue was added to give a bit of colour to the white. As I explained in the chapter about filters painters use the colour blue to help give a cold feeling to the tones.

For this example I applied the winter wash starting with the hull front and sides. Personally I like to focus on one part of the subject at a time when using the hairspray technique. While masking details such as the fenders, I airbrushed thicker coats of white into the corners. I airbrushed lighter amounts of the winter camo toward the outer more exposed areas that are susceptible to wear from the crew and infantry.

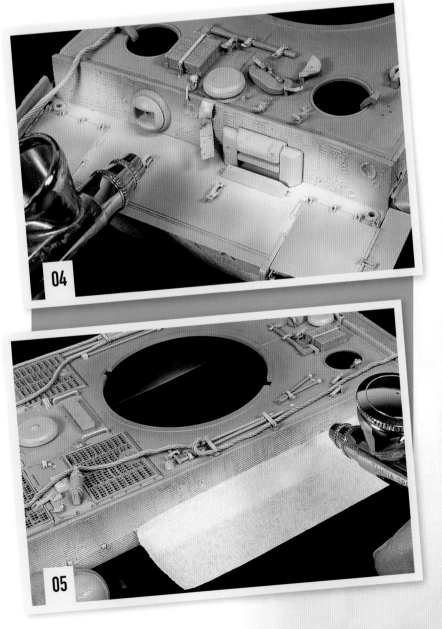

PHOTO 6 AND 7:

Tamiya paint when thinned with water dries quickly. You can immediately start carefully removing the paint using a modified stiff-bristled paint brush dampened with water. The water will moisten the hairspray allowing it to be removed along with the paint that is over it. You will see that the paint will come off resulting in smaller chips on the thicker coats of white.

You need to be more careful when chipping areas with thin amounts of white. You will find that the paint can be removed much easier from these areas resulting in larger chips. You can also use finer brushes and toothpicks to remove the layers of white.

Photo seven shows the different effects that will result on both the thick and thinner layers of paint over the hairspray. Thinner coats of white were applied over the fenders creating contrast between these parts and the thicker layers on the hull. This is a good example of using a winter camouflage to create distinction between parts.

PHOTO 8 AND 9:

Next I moved onto the top of the hull. Again note the different looking chipping effects over the various thick and thin layers of Tamiya white

PHOTO 10 :

The fenders on the hull sides were the last detail that I applied the winter camo to. I airbrushed a very light coat of white onto the fenders keeping the effect milder than that of the hull.

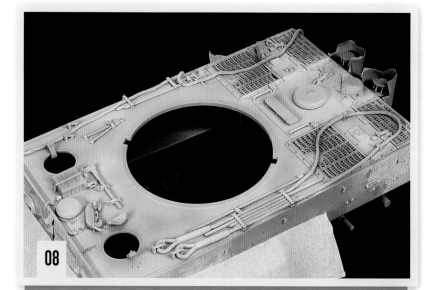

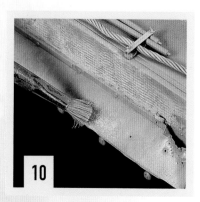

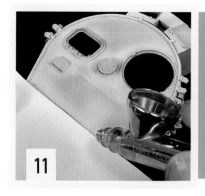
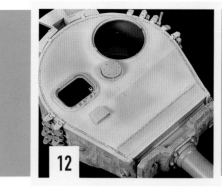
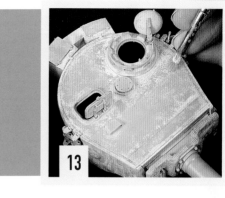

PHOTO 11 THROUGH 13:

I repeated the steps over the turret by first airbrushing two to three good coats of hairspray followed by a random coat of white paint. Paper was used to mask each of the plates. Applying different amounts of white between each of these details will allow for dissimilar chipping effects creating contrast. I kept the cupola apart from the turret during this step for ease of handling while also making different chipping effects than those seen on the rest of the turret. The cupola would be glued in place after the model was weathered.

PHOTO 14 AND 15:

Once I got the winter wash chipped to my liking I sealed the layer of hairspray and Tamiya paint with a few coats of matt varnish. This coat will prevent the white layer of Tamiya paint from being removed throughout the remaining weathering steps.

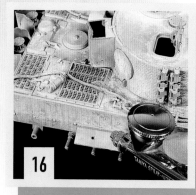

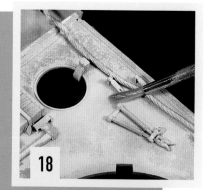

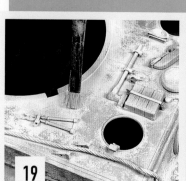

PHOTO 16 THROUGH 20:

You can build up effects over each other using multiple layers of hairspray and paint. After letting the first coat of hairspray, paint and varnish set for about three hours I continued by airbrushing another few good coats of hairspray over the model.

After applying another coat of white I chipped it in the same manner as the first with the aid of different paint brushes. You can see in photo 20 that two layers of hairspray and chipped paint will result in a more authentic looking white wash containing different intensities. I could have applied a third coat of hairspray, paint and varnish but I felt the winter wash to be authentic enough.

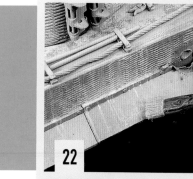

PHOTO 21 THROUGH 24:

Before sealing the second coat I added some runs using a paint brush over the hairspray with the same Tamiya white mix. Afterwards I removed areas of the runs with a modified stiff bristled brush.

PHOTO 25 THROUGH 27:
This time I sealed the model using a coat of Tamiya clear for the upcoming washes. Washes are easier to control when applied over satin and glossy surfaces. The oils used for the washes along with the other weathering effects will reduce this satin appearance as seen in the photos of the finished model.

A winter camouflage will add a lot of character and authenticity to a model. Remember to use it to help add contrast between parts and details. Keep in mind that you can build up layers of the winter camo if necessary in order to create an authentic result. Just let the coats of hairspray, paint and varnish dry for at least three to four hours prior to applying the next coat. More examples of using the hairspray technique to obtain different effects will be covered throughout this book.

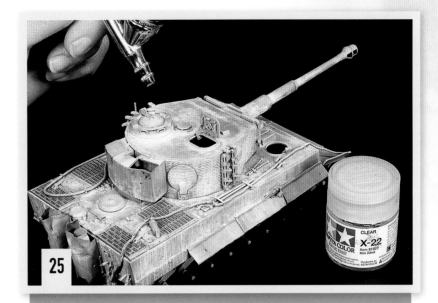

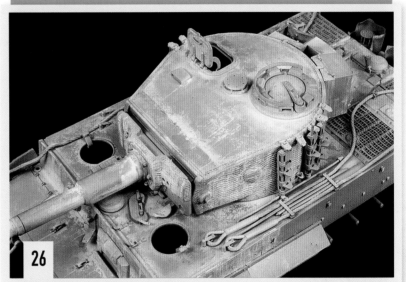

08

WASHES

MODELLERS HAVE BEEN USING WASHES AS A WAY OF ENHANCING DETAILS ON REPLICAS SINCE LONG BEFORE I WAS INVOLVED WITH THE HOBBY.

They are a quick means of adding subtle fake shadows and tonal variations. Washes will help to highlight details such as rivets, seams and textures. Like filters, washes also add more tones to a finish.

Applying washes is usually the first weathering step after a base coat if no filters are needed. In fact, even today some armour modellers prefer washes as the only weathering step needed to finish a model. Washes are usually a mix of around 15% paint and 85% thinner. The percentages of a mix can differ depending on where and why the wash is being applied. In this section we will look various techniques for applying washes. Washes will be used in conjunction with other finishing techniques throughout this book.

You can use most types of pants to make washes. I prefer oil and enamel paints because they have a slower drying time. There are a lot of oil paints on the market. I would encourage you to try different types for washes and other finishing techniques while also realising that the most expensive brands of oils are not

necessarily the best for finishing models. There are now also a lot of pre-mixed washes available in bottles that modellers can purchase. These products will aid beginners who are not yet confident with choosing and mixing their own colors. They are also quicker because no mixing or clean up is necessary.

Washes work best on glossy and satin surfaces.

A smooth glossy surface will allow the thinned paint to flow around the details creating fake shadows. On the contrary a general wash will act more like a filter on a matt surface as a result of the capillary action on this microscopic rough surface. Deferent techniques should be employed when applying washes over a matt surface then what is usualy needed for a glossy one. Let's begin with some examples of applying washes over satin and glossy surfaces.

WASHES OVER A SATIN SURFACE

IN THIS PART WE WILL BE PLACING WASHES OVER SOME DIFFERENT SATIN AND GLOSSY SURFACES.

I will also discuss the choice of colors to best use for these examples. You will see that although applying a wash is easier over a glossy or satin surface you should still keep an eye on the paint as it dries because some cleanup will be necessary.

 PHOTO 1 THROUGH 3:
Mixing colors for washes is important. I tend to mix dark grey-blue colors for vehicles in winter or rainy settings such as the pin washes being applied around the details of this Tiger I. I use dark brown colors on greens and over sand yellow finishes. Consideration should always be given to the colors that you mix for washes as they will affect the overall finish. A general wash applied to the whole model will also act like a filter.

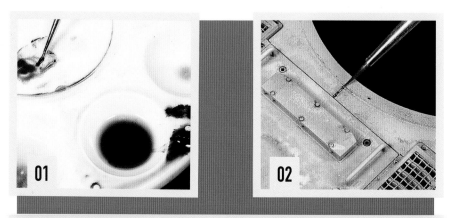

PHOTO 4:

When using thinned oil paints I tend to mix washes on an aluminum palette. In this case I filled two of the small trays with enamel thinner. I placed some brown oil paint on the tray and added small amounts at a time to the thinner. You can check the intensity of the wash by brushing some onto the pallet as shown. Sometimes I will simply mix thinner and oils together on the flat part of the pallet in order to obtain different ratios of paint-to-thinner for various parts of the model.

PHOTO 5 THROUGH 7:

Let's brush on some general washes. Surfaces are glossy because they are very smooth and that is why they reflect light. The thinned paint will tend to gather around details such as these bolts when the surface is smooth.

After brushing on a wash, wipe the brush onto a cloth or napkin then remove the excess thinner and paint from the model. In this case some of the paint will remain on the model resulting in a bit of a brown filter slightly darkening the camouflage.

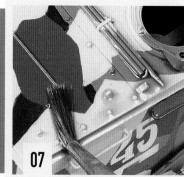

PHOTO 8 THROUGH 10:

After applying a general wash attention needs to be given ensuring that it dries properly. If you do not remove the excess wash from your model it could dry leaving an undesirable texture as seen in photo 8. Oil paints take a few days to dry. You should have plenty of time to remove some of this unattractive texture with a paintbrush dampened with thinner.

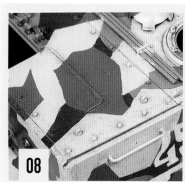

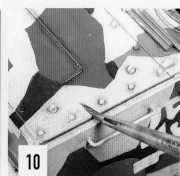

 PHOTO 11 THROUGH 14:
Let's look at another example of applying washes with this more complex 17 cm cannon. I applied a few coats of Tamiya X-22 clear over the basecoat and camouflage to obtain a good satin finish. Again I made a general wash and started applying it over the model.

 PHOTO 15 THROUGH 17:
Remove the excess wash from the part wiping it away on a piece of cloth or dinner napkin.

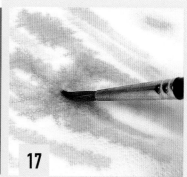

PHOTO 18 THROUGH 21:

The effect around the rivets in photo 18 is another example of what happens when you apply too much of the wash over an area. As the wash starts to dry simply touch up these parts using a brush dampened with turpentine than wiping the excess paint away on a cloth.

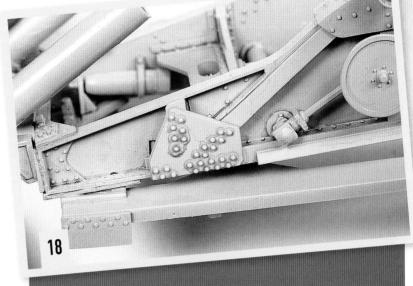

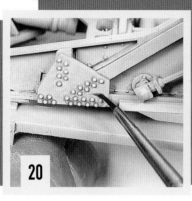

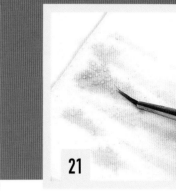

PHOTO 22 AND 23:

The result in photo 22 is the effect of a surface containing a basecoat with a slightly rougher texture. These differences in texture on a satin surface are a result of improper airbrushing technique. The capillary action of the texture pulled the thinned paint away from the rivets. As before you can blend this unwanted effect before it dries using a brush dampened with turpentine.

PHOTO 24 THROUGH 26:

The fenders on this LVT are another example of applying too much wash over a surface. Once the thinner starts to dry you can remove the excess paint using a brush.

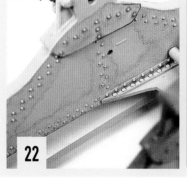

27

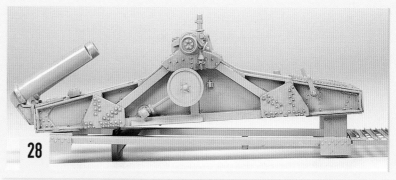

28

29

PHOTO 27:
You can also simply blend the oils once the thinner evaporates using a dry brush cleaning areas where you find the effects of the wash undesirable

PHOTO 28 AND 29:
Brushing the general wash onto a model or detail is one part of the technique. Equally important is watching the wash dry, touching up areas where needed.

PHOTO 30 THROUGH 33:
After the general washes are dry you can start adding localized washes, or "pin washes", into seams and around other details to obtain further shadows. Pin washes are a great means for distinguishing the different components from each other.

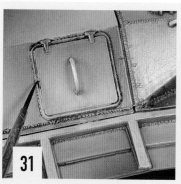

31

32

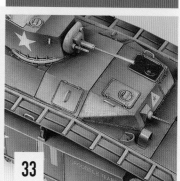

33

30

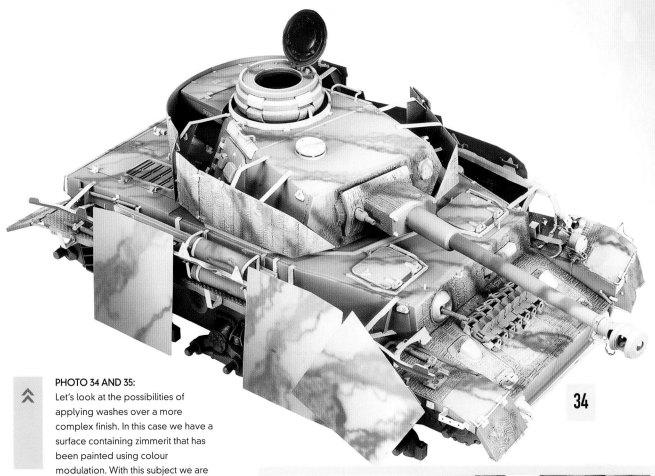

34

PHOTO 34 AND 35:

Let's look at the possibilities of applying washes over a more complex finish. In this case we have a surface containing zimmerit that has been painted using colour modulation. With this subject we are dealing with both light and shadowed regions. Therefore I mixed three different washes. These washes were a light brown, darker brown and a black one for the very dark areas.

PHOTO 36 THROUGH 38:

Zimmerit surfaces are very jagged. Rough surfaces like these will absorb the wash very quickly. If you are not careful a heavy wash will darken a surface containing zimmerit much more than if it had a smooth exterior.

To avoid this problem I applied the lighter brown wash over the areas containing zimmerit. The darker brown wash that I normally use was applied to all of the areas without zimmerit such as on the upper hull and turret. The final step was to carefully add some black washes into the shadowed areas.

35

36

37

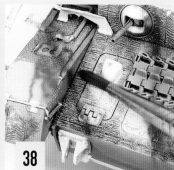

38

WASHES OVER A MATT SURFACE

IN ESSENCE THE TECHNIQUES USED WHEN APPLYING WASHES ONTO A SURFACE WITH A MATT FINISH ARE THE SAME AS USED ON A SATIN OR GLOSSY ONE

As I discussed earlier, the capillary action of the minuscule rough surface on this type of finish will make controlling washes more difficult. In this example we will first add a general wash over the model then use refined pin washes to help highlight seams, bolts and other details.

01

PHOTO 1 THROUGH 3:
I decided to thin the enamel wash that I was using further in order to avoid darkening the model too much. On my palette I filled one of the trays with the wash and two others with thinner. The first tray of thinner was used to mix a less dense wash. The second tray of thinner would be for cleaning the brush.

02

03

PHOTO 4 AND 5:
Although it would act more as a filter because of the matt surface, I first applied a general wash over the entire model in order to start highlighting details and seams. I also wanted to emphasize the minute casting textures on both the turret and hull.

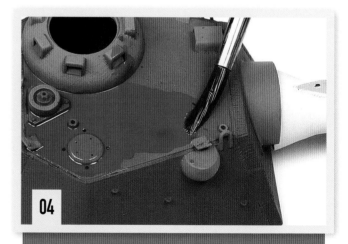

04

PHOTO 6:
After the first wash had about an hour to dry I started adding pin washes. Using a fine brush I placed the same mix into all of the seams, corners, holes and around other details. Just place the wet brush inside of a seam and capillary action will pull the wash in.

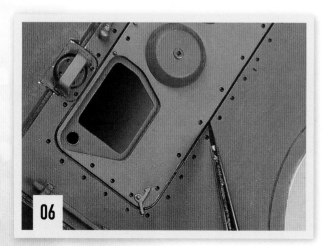

05

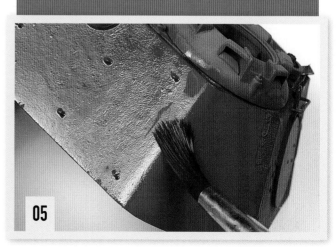

06

PHOTO 7 AND 8:
Photo seven shows how the capillary action of the matt surface can pull the thinned paint from the seam if too much is applied or if you miss the joint with your brush. In this case you need to let the paint set for a few minutes then blend it using a brush dampened with clean thinner.

PHOTO 9 THROUGH 12:
Placing a wash around details such as these vents can be tricky because the matt surface will pull the paint away from the seam were its supposed to be. To remove this paint simply take some clean thinner and start blending it away from the detail, slowly working it over to the unwanted paint, then removing it.

PHOTO 13 THROUGH 15:
The excess wash around these weld details was cleaned in the same manner

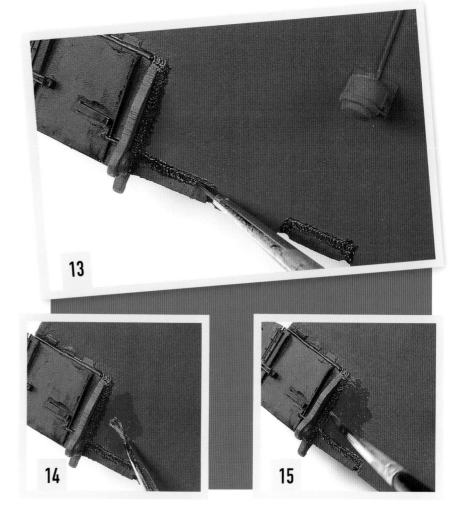

13

14

15

PHOTO 16 THROUGH 19:
After applying enamel washes and letting them dry random satin areas will be visible. These spots are sometimes referred to by modellers as "tide marks" and they are more common with enamels. On a satin or glossy surface tide marks are usually difficult to see but are much more evident on a matt face. The easiest way to reduce these effects is to airbrush a few coats of matt onto the model, particularly over the pin washes, after the enamels have had a day or so to dry.

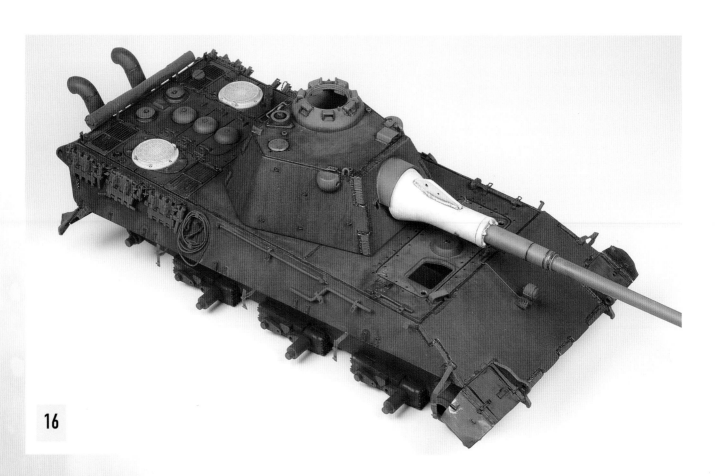

16

I actually find it more enjoyable and even therapeutic to apply washes over a model with a matt surface than one which has a satin finish. Although more difficult to control, pin washes are easy to blend and clean after they have had a few minutes to dry. You can see how pin washes really help to break up and bring out the different parts and details of a model.

After applying all of the washes there are still some techniques that can be added to give further tones to the finish and contrast amongst details. The next chapter entitled, "Fading and Adding Shadows" will cover these steps on some more different examples.

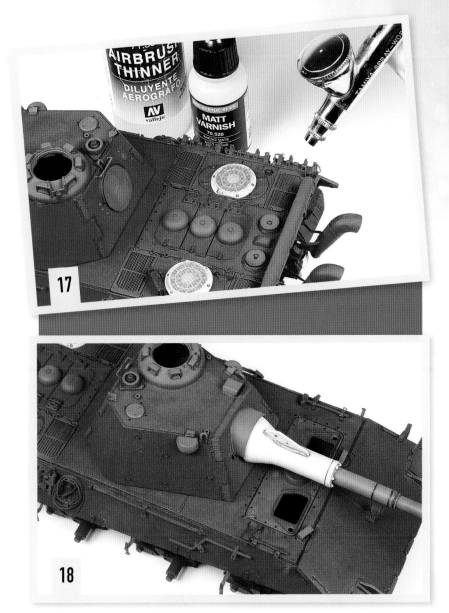

09 FADING AND ADDING SHADOWS

IN THE LAST SECTION I DEMONSTRATED HOW WASHES ARE USED TO CREATE SUBTLE SHADOWS ENHANCING DETAILS.

We also know that washes add more tones to the base coat. There are other methods available that can be used in conjunction with washes to add yet more dramatic shadows and tones creating further contrast amongst parts. The 30,5cm SFL Bär in these two images is a good example. Note the subtle yellow and light grey tones breaking the side, rear and upper plates of the superstructure. You can also see the brown tone blended into the corners of the top plate and protruding mantlet. Fading and adding shadows are fun techniques allowing the modeller more creative freedom with the overall finish. After all of the weathering these effects will be evident but less obvious. This is very important to remember as you will always need to balance your effects depending on what you will want the overall finish to look like.

Oil paints are normally used for fading and adding shadows although enamels and acrylics can also be employed. Oil paints are ideal for these steps because they dry very slowly allowing you plenty of time to blend them to your liking. Oil paints also dry to a matt finish after they set reducing a glossy varnish. As mentioned, there are lots of oil paints on the market with very similar properties. Experiment with different types remembering that the most expensive products are not necessarily the best.

The first examples will show some simple methods for fading and adding shadows that can be applied over monotone finishes. With the second part of this section we will be employing the same techniques but a bit more dramatically over a complex camouflage.

ADDING SHADOWS AND FADING ON A SINGLE TONE FINISH

FOR THE FIRST EXAMPLE I WILL DEMONSTRATE BOTH FADING AND ADDING SHADOWS TO THE HULL OF THIS JS-3 SOVIET TANK.

As you can see this model contains a green finish with faint colour modulation. The subtle fading and shadows applied to a base coat containing a single tone finish can be quick and easy. Let's look at this example.

PHOTO 1 THROUGH 5:
After mixing a brown tone I started outlining details like the weld seams and fenders. Next I cleaned the brush in enamel thinner, wiped it on a napkin, and started blending the brown lines.

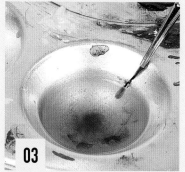

PHOTO 6 THROUGH 10:
I dried the brush completely by blowing it with air from my airbrush. With the paintbrush completely dry I finished blending the brown oil paints.

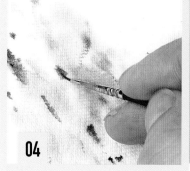

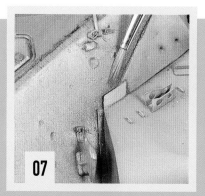

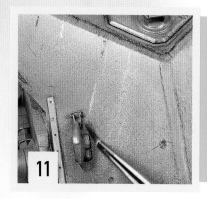

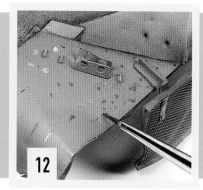

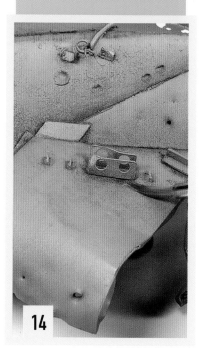

PHOTO 11 THROUGH 14:

Blending selected oil colors can help to add more subtle tones onto the base coat of a model. For this example I blended yellow, green and brown tones to enrich the base colour. Conversely you can use lighter grey tones and white to fade a colour. This is why modellers refer to adding oils in the manner as, "fading". It depends upon the subject that you are painting and what you want to end up with. Fading in essence is a type of filter as discussed earlier. Use a vertical blending motion on the sides of the vehicle and employ a tapping motion on the horizontal planes of the model such as the tops of these fenders.

PHOTO 15:

In photo 15 we can see the following effects on the hull. First washes have been applied as discussed earlier to add subtle shadows hi-lighting details such as bolts and seams. Next, brown oils were blended to create more dramatic shadows generating further contrast around weld seams and the bigger details such as the fenders and other sheet metal components. Thirdly I blended bits of green, yellow and brown over the different surfaces of the model to enrich the green creating more subtle tones while subtly blending the colour modulation.

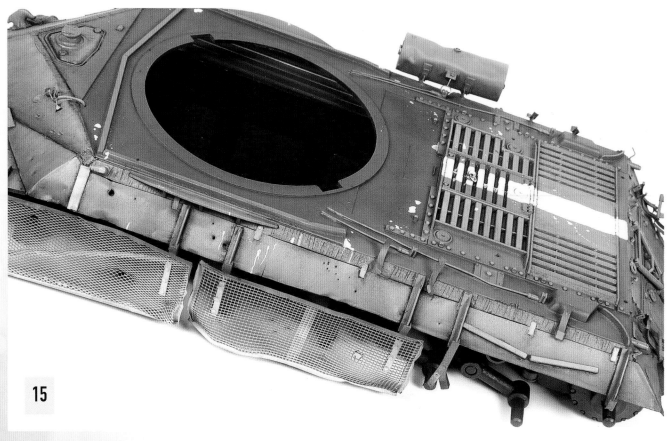

16

17

18

PHOTO 16 THROUGH 18:
In the example of the LVT I resulted to lighter grays and blues to add more tones.

PHOTO 19 AND 20:
Remember that after blending the oils you can spread them further and more evenly using a dry brush without any thinner.

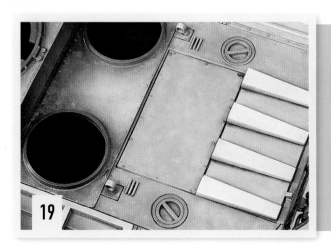

19

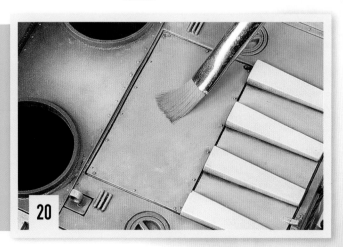

20

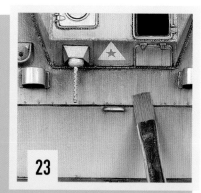

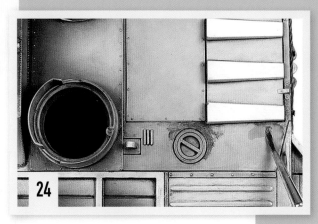

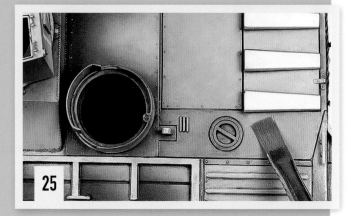

PHOTO 21 THROUGH 26:
As a result of operating in salt water this completed LVT would contain a large amount of rust tones. I took this moment to blend some more brown oils that would add further contrast but also act as a base for the anticipated rust tones that would be applied later on.

PHOTO 27 THROUGH 29:
As with filters and washes you will discover that oils blend a bit differently over matt surfaces. To start with I used red, yellow and brown oils to add more subtle tones to the primer red colour of this E-50. Brown shadows were blended around the cupola. This is one example of the advantages for keeping parts unglued until the model is completed. An orange colour was used to break apart the front and rear plates from the sides of the turret.

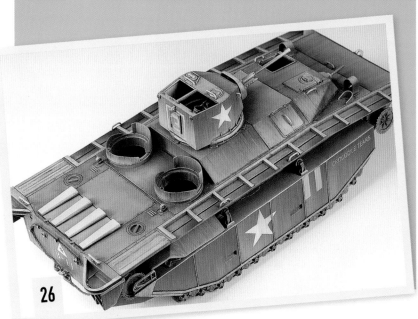

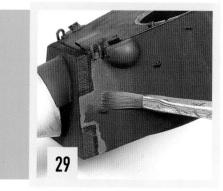

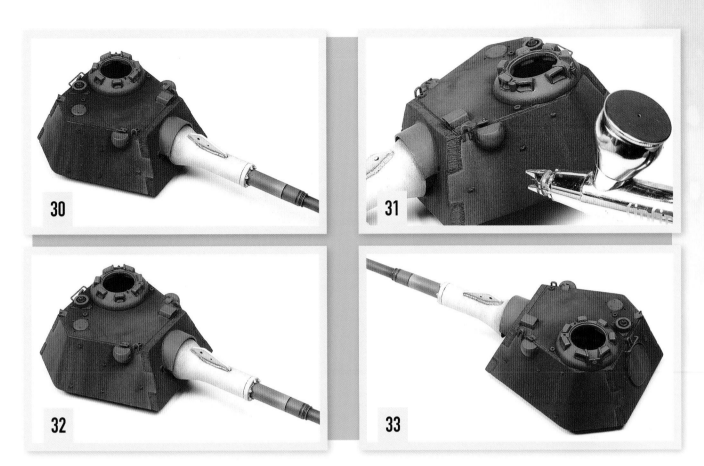

PHOTO 30 THROUGH 34:

It is more difficult to blend oils over a matt surface because of its minute rough structure. After finishing this step I felt the orange tones to be too intense. In order to reduce this effect seen on the sides of the turret in photo 30 I airbrushed some faint amounts of the base coat over these areas. Again, it is always good to keep some extra amounts of the basecoat mix on hand for subtle touch ups as seen here.

Because of the colour modulation the shadows created in this section took on more of a supportive role in adding contrast to the JS-3, LVT and E-50 models. The JSU in the next example contains a rather complex camouflage making the use of colour modulation more difficult. For that case I would need to depend only on the washes fading and shadows to

add more contrast amongst its different details. Although more of a review after this section, I'll further demonstrate the potential of these techniques.

FADING AND ADDING SHADOWS OVER A CAMOUFLAGE

DURING THIS EXAMPLE WE WILL BE ADDING SHADOWS AND FADING EFFECTS ONTO A RATHER VIBRANT CAMOUFLAGE.

These effects will work in conjunction with the washes applied earlier to help break up the different details on the replica despite the strong camouflage. You will see that the techniques used are pretty much the same as applied in the previous section.

 PHOTO 1 THROUGH 3:
After mixing a dark-brown colour I broke the model down into imaginary parts and started outlining details as shown.

02

01

03

PHOTO 4 AND 5:

Next I started blending the oils using a paint brush dampened with enamel thinner. After blending another brush completely dry of any thinner was used to finish merging the tone.

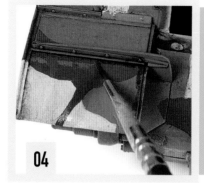

PHOTO 6 THROUGH 17:

Photos six through 17 display more examples of where I blended oils to create face shadows and contrast between parts.

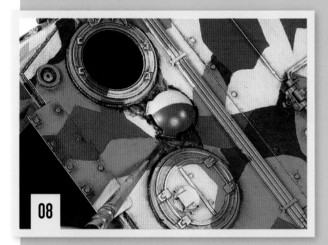

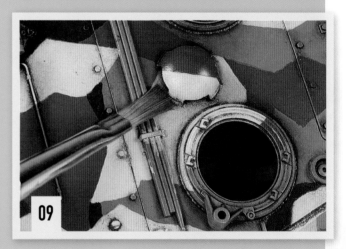

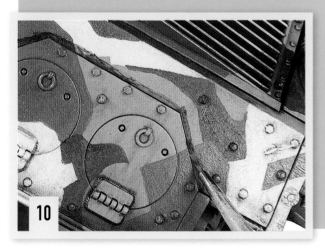

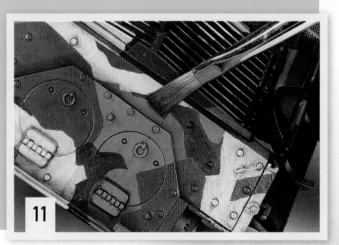

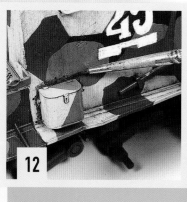

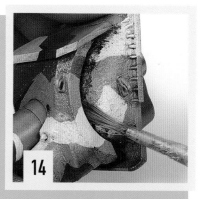

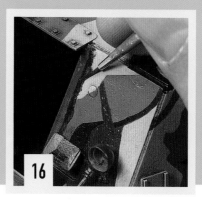

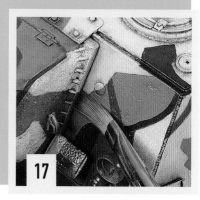

PHOTO 18 AND 19:
Different coloured oils were blended over the surfaces of the model to add more tones while subtly blending the camouflage. The colors blended were primarily a buff with a touch of brown.

PHOTO 20:
Use a tapping motion to blend the oils on horizontal surfaces.

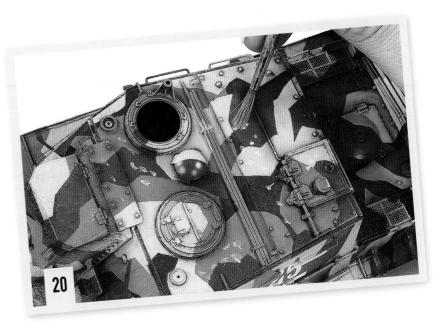

PHOTO 21 AND 22:
Photos 21 and 22 show the JSU-152 after all of the oil techniques were applied. You can see that the washes applied initialy also work in conjunction with the shadows and fading helping to distinguish each of the sections and details of the model despite its complex camouflage.

At this stage we are now ready to move onto replicating chips and flaws in the paint. Armour modellers simply refer to these techniques as "chipping". Chipping is more of a process as it involves a number of techniques. It can be very tedious but if applied properly chipping can really enhance the authenticity of your model. Lets again move forward with some different examples of chipping.

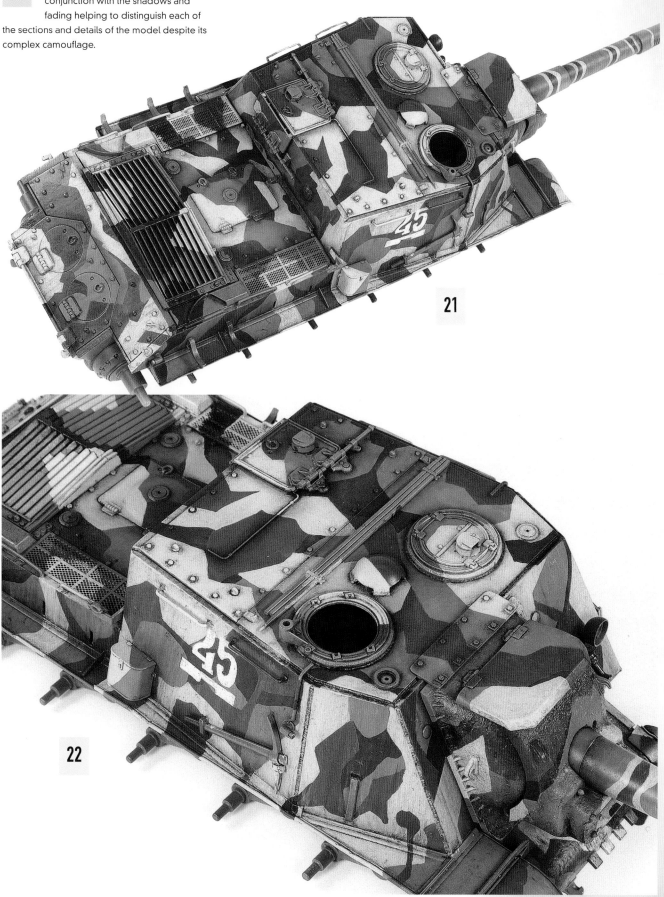

10 PAINT CHIPPING EFFECTS

AFTER WORKING WITH OIL PAINTS ON THE FINISH OF A REPLICA I USUALLY START THE CHIPPING STEPS.

Modellers refer to chipping as replicating chips, scratches and other flaws in the paint. These flaws are supposedly caused form impacts, fragments, weathering and the crew. Chipping can be very tedious but if all of the different steps are applied properly chipping, like some other important techniques, can really enhance the authenticity of your model while also creating contrast between details. Therefore I take these steps very seriously and have made the chipping process a signature step in the work I publish.

In this section I have some different examples for creating chipping effects. The first approach is the more common method of carefully painting

chips over the basecoat and camouflage using practices such as a sponge and/or a fine paintbrush. Modellers now refer to this way of creating chips as, "the traditional method" because hairspray has also become a popular means for this task.

The second approach that I will demonstrate is the hairspray technique explained in the chapter about applying a winter white wash, this method can also be used to make chipping effects. This method is more popular with modellers when they are finishing old rusty wrecked and burnt out AFVs but fine chips can also made with this method. Let's begin with some examples of creating chips using a fine paintbrush.

CHIPPING WITH A SPONGE AND PAINT BRUSH

I FIND THAT THE TRADITIONAL METHOD OF CHIPPING USING A SPONGE AND FINE BRUSH IN CONJUNCTION WITH OTHER TECHNIQUES STILL ALLOWS FOR

THE BEST CONTROL WHEN REPLICATING FINE FLAWS ON PAINT THAT LOOK TO SCALE.

This segment will contain four examples of using the traditional chipping process. First we continue with the JSU-152 to demonstrate a

regular example of chipping effects that I apply onto most of the models that I finish. Second we will be creating heavy chips onto the side of an LVT. For the third part I will show an example of painting heavy chips and scratches onto the exterior of a set of Panzer IV Schürzen. In the fourth part we will look at applying chipping effects onto Zimmerit surfaces.

STANDARD CHIPPING

THE CHIPPING PROCESSES THAT I USE IS MADE UP FROM A NUMBER OF TECHNIQUES.

I will use a few different models to show chipping using a sponge and fine brush. I will also demonstrate other very important methods such as speckling and applying rust tones that should also be applied with chipping effects. All of these techniques can be used together resulting in a very authentic appearance. The method of blending graphite to give a metallic shine over areas containing lots of chips is also important to the process but should be applied after weathering. I will discuss using graphite to enhance chipping and metal surfaces later.

It can be very easy to overdo chipping. A fine, hi-quality new brush is most important. Your paint also needs to be thinned properly. You should be relaxed and focused.

Study reference photos beforehand. Sometimes the amounts, shapes and sizes of paint chips can differ greatly depending on the location, conflict and/or country where the vehicle was manufactured and used. The shapes and sizes of chips can also differ greatly on various parts of an AFV such as this T-55 recovery vehicle. Note the differences in the sizes and intensities of the

chips when comparing the lower hull, fenders and hatches to each other. The photos of the Syrian T-55 that I studied when painting this replica was camouflaged more than once using civilian paint. The chips on different parts of this vehicle had come off in very large rounded shapes at different intensities. The worn camouflage on this T-64 frequently climbed on by museum visitors is another example of how large amounts of paint can be worn away over time. Viewing construction equipment can also be a great way of understanding chipping patterns.

The JSU-152 in this chapter represents an example of the level to which I perform chipping effects onto a standard armour model supposedly containing a factory finish. This is why I am referring to this part as "Standard Chipping". We will start by painting all of the large exposed metallic areas such as the hinges, hatch openings and the mounts for the external fuel tanks.

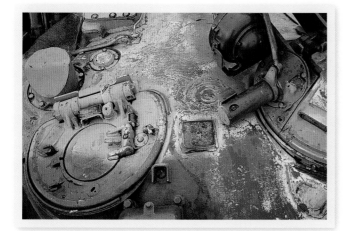

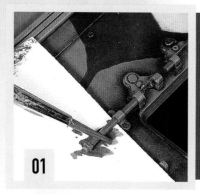

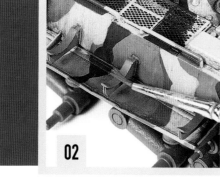

PHOTO 1 THROUGH 3:

To begin I usually mix a dark grey tone with acrylics thinned with a little water. I start painting details where large amounts of chipping or bare metal will be present. In this example these areas included mounts for the external fuel tanks and openings around the hatches.

PHOTO 4:

I usually continue the process using the sponge technique. A sponge allows you to quickly apply fine random chipping effects. In this example we will be applying chips of the green base coat supposedly evident through the camouflage colors. When you are applying chipping effects over layers of paint it is very important that that you match the colour with the base coat or the effects will look unconvincing. Acrylics such as Lifecolor and Vallejo work well for this step. Here I am matching the base colour of the suspension parts.

PHOTO 5 AND 6:

There are all kinds of sources for you to obtain sponges that can be used for chipping effects. Packing sponges usually work very well. Just get a large portion and rip off small pieces as you need it. Cut away the jagged edges creating a nice circular shape that you can easily hold using a set of tweezes.

PHOTO 7 THROUGH 10:

It very important that you first remove all of the excess paint from the sponge onto a piece of paper before using it to replicate paint chips on the model. You only want it to press the sponge lightly leaving very fine chips. On this JSU-152 I applied the base green chips onto the camouflage colors where large amounts of chips in the paint might be present. These areas included the corners, fenders and other exposed components subject to wear and tear.

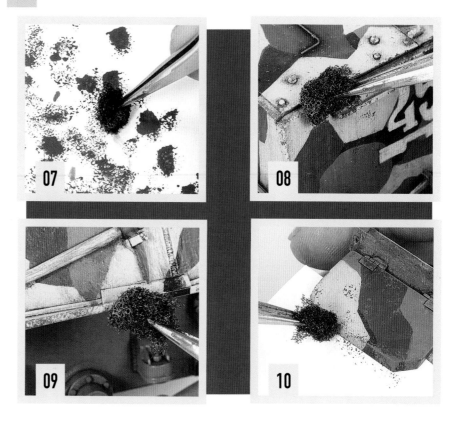

PHOTO 11:

The sponge can be a quick means for applying chips on small details such as tool clamps and cable mounts. In this case tape was employed to keep the chips confined only to the mounts and away from the hull of this Tiger I. Small exposed details such as these are sometimes more prone to chipping.

PHOTO 12 THROUGH 14:

Now it was time to start adding more controlled chips using a paint brush. I carefully mixed a green that matched the basecoat using acrylics. I thinned the colour to about the consistency of milk using water. Thin the paint until the mixture is almost falling from the brush in drops when you remove it from the pallet.

Equally important is your paint brush. I usually use a Winsor & Newtan Series Seven 000 Sable for this task. Although more costly these brushes will keep a nice pointed tip for quite a while allowing you to obtain very fine controlled chips.

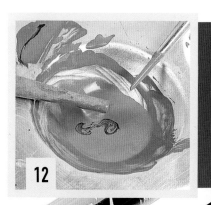

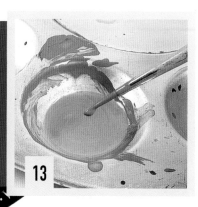

PHOTO 15:

After dipping the brush first wipe the excess paint away onto a piece of paper.

PHOTO 16 THROUGH 19:

Do not try to draw the chips but instead use a light tapping motion with the brush. Make sure that your brush is always perpendicular to the surface of the model. During this step apply larger chips over the finer ones created by the sponge giving a more random authentic looking effect.

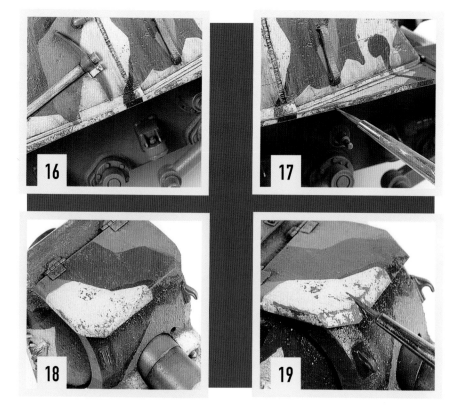

PHOTO 20 AND 21:

Add larger chips onto metal surfaces where lots of chipping will be evident. On this example these areas include places where removable components are mounted such as the exterior fuel tanks. Finer flexible sheet metal details such as strapping will also contain a lot of chipping effects.

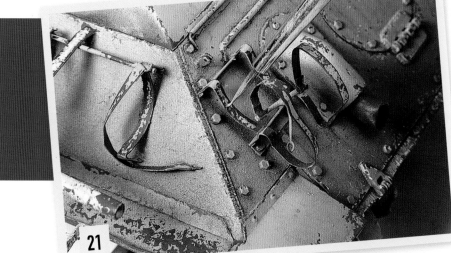

PHOTO 22:

After applying the chips by brush, thin the acrylic paint further so you can add subtle scratches over the camouflage.

23 **24** **25**

PHOTO 23 THROUGH 25:

Next I mixed another shade of green lighter than the base green colour. These chips where to represent fresh layers of scraped paint. Again, starting with the sponge I added light green chips onto all of the green areas of the finish.

PHOTO 26:

A sponge is also great for quickly creating large numbers of chips on details where the paint might receive lots of wear such as the running gear. These details usually end up getting mostly covered with weathering effects and earth tones. It is sometimes unnecessary to devote much time to details such as these with tedious effects such as chipping with a fine brush.

26

27 **28** **29**

PHOTO 27 THROUGH 29:

Again the light green chips created with the sponge were touched up using a fine brush. As with the green lighter shades of sand yellow and brown chips were added to these camouflage tones.

PHOTO 30 AND 31:

At this point I was ready to add dark brown steel chips. Like with the green chips I thinned the paint to about the consistency of milk. A little sand was added to lighten the tone resulting in a softer contrast between the dark brown and the rest of the colors.

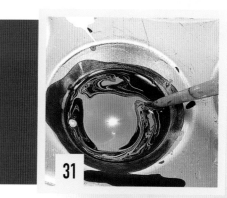

30 **31**

PHOTO 32 THROUGH 36:
After wiping the excess paint from the brush I added brown chips over much, but not all, of the lighter tones applied in the previous chipping steps. You can see in photos 35 and 36 that there are a number of different coloured chips working together adding authenticity to the finish. Adding chips to a complex camouflage like this can be tedious and time consuming but the results are well worth the effort.

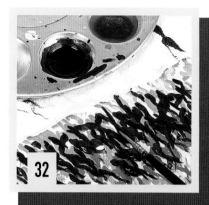

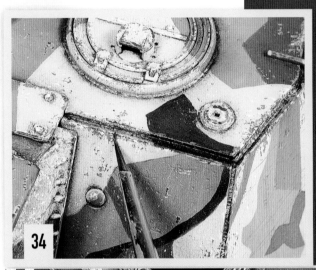

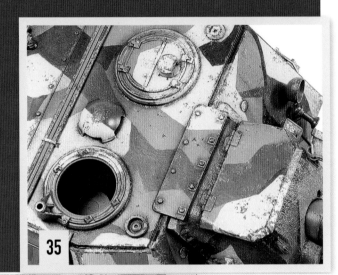

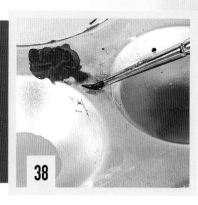

PHOTO 37 AND 38:
Now it was time to add some rust over the areas containing lots of chips. I mixed a few rust tones using enamels, oil paints and pigments. Mixing oils with enamels will give you some of the blending capabilities of oils. The mix will also contain the opaque properties of the enamel while also drying a bit quicker. The pigments are for added colour. Enamel thinner was used to dilute the mix prior to placing it onto the model.

PHOTO 39 THROUGH 43:
You can paint the rust tone onto the areas with larger chips then blend it with enamel thinner. You can also thin the mix and apply the tone as a localized wash.

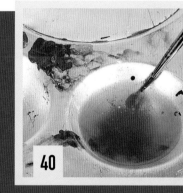

PHOTO 44 THROUGH 45:
You do not need to apply the rust tone to all of the chips.

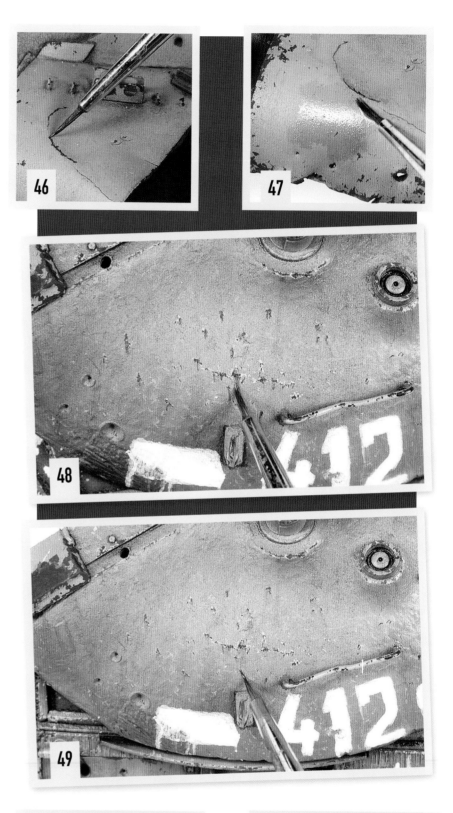

>> **PHOTO 46 THROUGH 49:**
The next four photos show some more examples of blending rust tones over chips and scrapes on this JS-3. You can see that this is a very subtle effect. Operating vehicles like this were not often in the field long enough to accumulate large amounts of rust.

>> **PHOTO 50 AND 51:**
IThick dark rust washes were also blended over the large chipped areas containing lots of exposed metal.

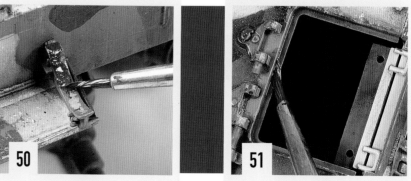

PHOTO 52 THROUGH 56:
Now it was time to add some more very fine chips of dark rust using the speckling technique. To perform this step I needed a modified stiff bristled brush. The same rust tones mixed for the previous step were used. I removed the excess paint from the brush then tested the result by flicking specks of paint onto a clean piece of paper. Once I am content with the outcome I carefully speckled fine amounts of rust over the model.

PHOTO 57 AND 58:
Again focus most of the rust specks onto areas where the most chips are present. Use paper or tape to mask places where you want less speckles. Tape was used to mask areas around the damaged hatch of this Tiger I stowage bin.

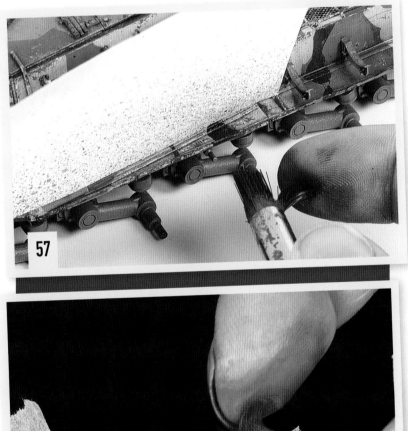

PHOTO 59 THROUGH 62:
After the speckling I decided to add more runs of rust onto some of the areas of the superstructure and gun.

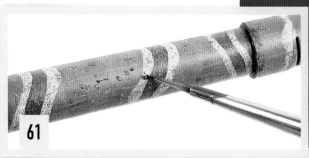

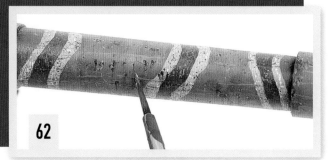

PHOTO 63 THROUGH 65:
Runs of dark grey were also blended to areas under the gun.

Although time consuming and tedious the importance of effectively carrying out the chipping steps is apparent on this JSU-152. Evident through most of the weathering, chipping works in conjunction with the earth tones giving a final authentic result to your model.

LIST OF STEPS

Below is a list of steps that I applied to complete the chipping process on this JSU-152. I have also listed the steps applied onto the JS-3. Again, these are a few examples of how I carry out the chipping steps on most of the models I complete. Sometimes the chipping will be more or less intense depending on the subject and how long it's been in the field. Please note that you will often need to go back and forth between the different steps on order to obtain a result that you feel is convincing. Also keep in mind that these steps do not necessarily need to be applied in the same order.

JSU-152 (CONTAINING A CAMOUFLAGE)

1) Brushing grey tones over steel areas.

2) Adding green chips over the camouflage using a sponge.

3) Adding more controlled green chips and scratches over the camouflage with a fine paintbrush.

4) Applied lighter green chips over areas of the green base coat using a sponge.

5) Paint more light green chips and scratches over the green using a brush.

6) Adding lighter shades of chips and scrapes over the camouflage colors using a brush.

7) Put on dark brown rust chips using a brush.

8) Blended thinned amounts of rust tones over areas containing lots of chips.

9) Speckling with fine amounts of rust.

JS-3

1) Brushing grey tones over steel areas.

2) Adding fine light green chips using a sponge.

3) Adding more controlled light green chips and scratches using a brush.

4) Blended thinned amounts of rust tones over areas containing lots of chips.

5) Speckling fine amounts of light green.

6) Speckling fine amounts of rust.

LARGE CHIPS USING A BRUSH

ALTHOUGH THE HAIRSPRAY TECHNIQUE HAS BECOME MORE COMMON FOR CREATING HEAVY LARGE CHIPPING EFFECTS ON SCALE MODELS IT CAN STILL SOMETIMES BE SIMPLER AND QUICKER TO USE A PAINT BRUSH FOR OBTAINING THESE TYPES OF EFFECTS.

In this example we will make some large areas of chips that I observed in reference photos on the sides of this LVT using the same techniques covered earlier. Again, the paint brush that you choose along with properly thinning the acrylic paints is very important. As always a few techniques will be needed to obtain the final result.

PHOTO 1 AND 2:
To start, the basic shapes of the large brown chips were painted onto the sides of the model using a 00 Winsor & Newton series 7 paint brush.

PHOTO 3 AND 4:
Next I randomly painted a dark grey colour onto the large brown chips in order to start getting some variations in the rust. I also outlined the edges of the chips using a lighter tone of the base coat.

PHOTO 5 AND 6:
Another rust tone mixed from Humbrol enamels and pigments was applied over the chipped areas and blended using thinner.
This step blended and worked with the brown and dark grey acrylics while adding further matt rust tones.

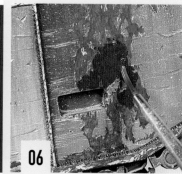

07

08

PHOTO 7 THROUGH 9:
The same enamel mix was used to add random heavy runs of rust over different parts of the vehicle.

As I just showed you in this example sometimes applying large chips by brush can be quicker and simpler then when using hairspray. Again we utilized a number of steps using various rust tones in order to get the final result. Next we will

do another example of heavy chipping onto the side skirts of a panzer IV. Again we will be using traditional brush techniques over the base coat in conjunction with a few new steps for obtaining heavy scratches.

09

HEAVY CHIPPING (SCHÜRZEN)

IN THIS THIRD CASE I WANTED TO SHOW ANOTHER, MORE EXTREME, EXAMPLE OF CHIPPING.

Exposed details such as these Panzer IV schürzen were subject to a lot of wear especially if the vehicle had been in the field for a substantial amount of time. Some of the methods used for this instance will be more of a review from earlier with a few new techniques used in order to help create some different types of scratches and chips.

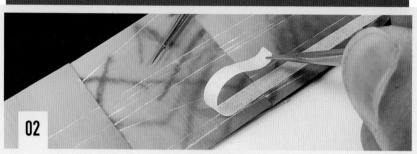

PHOTO 1 AND 2:
The first thing that I decided to do was paint some large scratches using thinned oil paints. Tamiya tape was employed to aid in obtaining straight lines.

PHOTO 3 THROUGH 6:
Next I needed to make all of the fine scratches evident in my reference photo. I accomplished this task using a modified flat jagged brush. A light sand tone was mixed using Vallejo acrylics. Wipe the excess paint from the brush onto a piece of paper and first apply the scratches onto a test piece to see if you are happy with the result prior to performing the technique on your model.

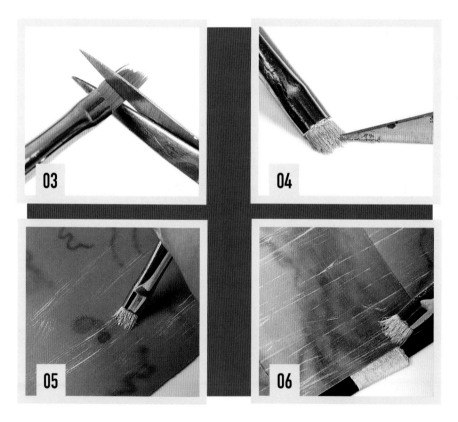

PHOTO 7 AND 8:
Light sand chips again mixed from Vallejo acrylics were applied using a fine brush. Do not forget to thin the paint using water as shown earlier. Next I applied a dark brown acrylic tone over a number of the lighter sand chips and scratches.

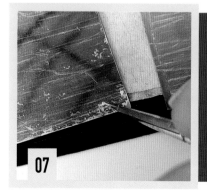

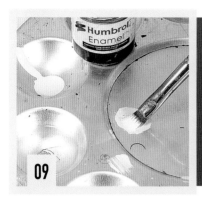
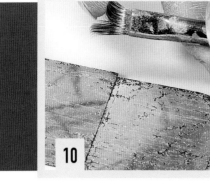
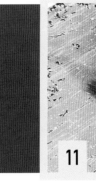

PHOTO 9 THROUGH 11:

More faint chips were added using the speckling technique. Remove some of the specs before the paint dries using a brush and enamel thinner if you feel that the effect is too much.

PHOTO 12 THROUGH 14:

After the specs had dried for a while some rust washes were blended over the areas containing lots of chips. The last step needed prior to weathering was to speckle on some more fine bits of rust.

This is an extreme example of chipping. I wanted to include this case because it quickly and clearly displays the different steps that I often use during the chipping process. Let's look at another example of chipping this time over a zimmerit surface.

CHIPPING ZIMMERIT

THE FORTH EXAMPLE THAT I WANT TO COVER IS APPLYING CHIPPING EFFECTS OVER A ZIMMERIT SURFACE.

Although the material and texture is different you will see that the techniques are pretty much the same.

PHOTO 1:
In photo one are a few pieces of actual zimmerit. The pieces toward your left show the tan colour of the paste. Note the maroon chips that are most likely bits of the red oxide paint that it was applied over. The pieces on the left display the dark yellow coat. Please note that this tone may be faded as a result of age.

PHOTO 2:
Zimmerit was applied over the primer. Therefore I first painted all of the large chips in the zimmerit with a primer red tone mixed from acrylics.

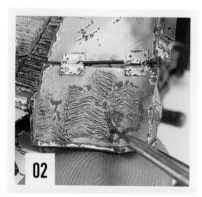

PHOTO 3 THROUGH 5:
A light tan tone was mixed from enamels and pigments and brushed over the primer red areas. Turpentine was used to blend and remove some of the tan paint. Blending the tan and reveling some of the primer looks like remnants of the zimmerit left over from where it had been chipped away.

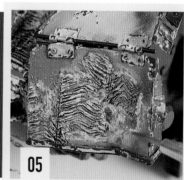

>> **PHOTO 6 AND 7:**
More chips were given to the zimmerit surfaces using another light tan tone this time mixed from acrylics.

>> **PHOTO 8 THROUGH 10:**
The last step prior to weathering was to add some faint chips and flaws over the sand tone using speckling.

06

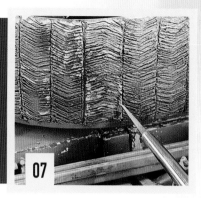

07

The Panzer IV used in the last two examples of this chapter contains rather heavy chipping. The extent to which you carry out the different techniques of the chipping depend upon the subject. I have demonstrated in this chapter that chipping with a brush is like most other finishing methods in that it should be applied in conjunction with other techniques. The sponge method, speckling and light rust tones also play an important role. Both thought and care should be given when applying each of these methods.

As I mentioned earlier, there is one more technique that is part of the chipping process.

Blending graphite over the larger chips will add a nice metallic sheen. This is one of the final steps that I apply because some of the upcoming wreathing steps would simply nullify the effect. Using graphite to enhance chipping will be discussed later in this chapter and in more detail at the end of the book.

08

09

10

PAINT CHIPPING USING HAIRSPRAY

ALTHOUGH STILL MORE COMMON FOR CREATING WINTER CAMOUFLAGES AND RUST EFFECTS, SOME MODELLERS ALSO PREFER HAIRSPRAY AS A MEANS OF OBTAINING FINE CHIPS ON THEIR MODELS.

In the next examples we will be using some of the same methods discussed earlier. In this part we will look at two examples to demonstrate what can be possible when using the hairspray technique to make fine chipping effects. In the first example we will make some fine chips on a sprocket.

For the second example we will use hairspray to help us create some small chips representing the remnants of zimmerit pattern on the side of a Tiger one. Let's get started.

STANDARD CHIPPING, HAIRSPRAY METHOD

THERE ARE NOW MANY PEOPLE WHOM PREFER THE HAIRSPRAY TECHNIQUE AS THE WAY TO CHIP THE ENTIRE MODEL.

This also includes fine chips like the ones that were applied by brush demonstrated earlier. I normally do not choose the hairspray method for fine chipping. This technique requires a single layer of colour to be airbrushed over a coat of hairspray that is on a dark base coat. Colour modulation for example has become a signature step in the models that I publish. Colour modulation uses multiple layers of paint making fine chipping with the hairspray technique difficult. I still do not get the same control with the hairspray method that I do when using a fine brush for obtaining chipping effects, but if you are familiar with using hairspray as a means of chipping you can really obtain some actual very fine chips that are extremely difficult to replicate using the finest of brushes. In this example I will perform some fine chipping with the aid of hairspray over these Friulmodel cast metal Tiger II drive sprockets.

01

» **PHOTO 1 AND 2:**
For this example I will use a red oxide primer colour as the basecoat. I added two to three coats of hairspray using quick passes with a spray can.

02

» **PHOTO 3 AND 4:**
I used Tamiya paints thinned with water for the coat of dark yellow. One rather light coat of paint is all that is needed. If you make this coat too thick it will be more difficult to remove the paint.

03

04

PHOTO 5 AND 6:

You also need to be careful with the amount of hairspray that you apply when chipping in this manner. If you apply too much fine cracking will result as seen in photo number five. I was able to make this example work but these cracks can still reduce the authenticity of the finished part. I applied only two quick coats of hairspray on the second drive sprocket instead of three and less cracking resulted.

PHOTO 7 AND 8:

Working on one wheel at a time I loaded some water into my airbrush and sprayed a coat over the first sprocket. Using a toothpick I started rubbing the paint from the part focusing on the corners. You will need to spray the water over the part a few times while performing this task.

PHOTO 9 AND 10:

Next I continued removing some of the paint using a damp modified paintbrush.

PHOTO 11 AND 12:

With the chipping complete a coat of clear was added to seal the outer layer of paint protecting it from the upcoming finishing steps. Lighter tones of the basecoat using Life Colour paints were added with a fine brush. These chips will represent where the sand yellow tone has been scraped.

You can also use this step to reduce the size of chips that you feel to be too large. This lighter tone can also cover areas where you accidently scraped through to the plastic or metal as in this case.

PHOTO 13 THROUGH 15:
A general wash was applied over the entire part. After about 15 minutes I applied some more pin washes to further bring out details. Once the washes were dry some more fine rust chips were added with speckling.

PHOTO 16 THROUGH 18:
I carefully removed the paint from the teeth of the sprocket using sandpaper exposing the metal underneath. Some graphite was lightly rubbed over the teeth and other areas to finish off the part.

Creating fine chips using hairspray can be a very powerful technique as it allows you to obtain very authentic scratches in the paint. As I have shown, this is another method that works best in conjunction with other techniques. Next we will see another example of obtaining fine chips and effects using hairspray this time to create the remnants of a zimmerit pattern.

REMNANTS OF A ZIMMERIT PATTERN

IN THIS PART WE WILL LOOK AT ANOTHER EXAMPLE OF MAKING CHIPPING EFFECTS USING THE HAIRSPRAY TECHNIQUE.

This time we are going to make an effect that represents chipped remnants of a zimmerit pattern where large patches of it have broken away from the hull. With careful masking and preparation you can keep effects using hairspray confined to specific areas. I also used the hairspray technique to add the winter wash described earlier. Please note that I resorted to the traditional methods of creating chipping effects over all of the sand yellow areas such as the hull, turret and fenders.

01

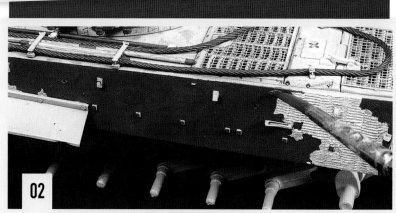

02

PHOTO 1 AND 2:
Continuing with the Tiger I as we left it earlier, the first thing needed was to paint all of the areas of chipped zimmerit by brush using a grey mild steel toned acrylic.

PHOTO 3 AND 4:
Next I masked everything using both tape and liquid mask. After I applied three to four good coats of hairspray using an airbrush.

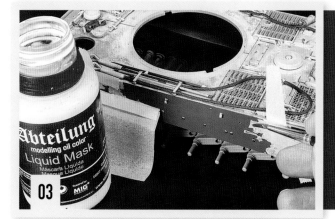

03

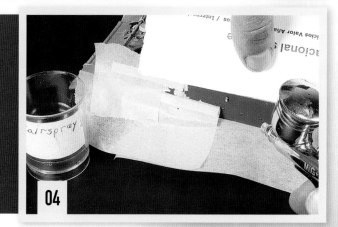

04

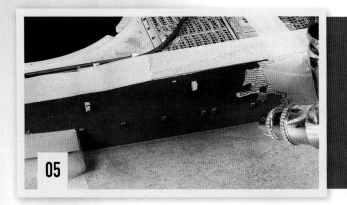

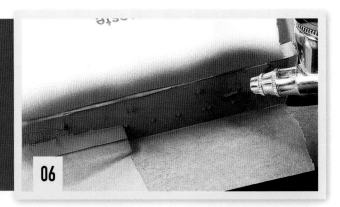

PHOTO 5 AND 6:

Over the hairspray I applied a few tones of primer red using Tamiya paints thinned with water. I started with a darker red-brown coat near the bottom then a lighter one towards the top. This was not so much as in attempt at colour modulation but more of a means of obtaining different tonal effects on the primer red once the chipping process was completed.

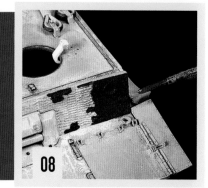

PHOTO 7 AND 8:

If you are quick you can also apply amounts of hairspray using a paintbrush. You need to be fast when applying the coat using only single passes because the hairspray, when manipulated too much, can lift away the acrylic paint. Next a coat of the primer tone was quickly brushed over the hairspray after it had dried again with a paintbrush using quick single passes.

PHOTO 9 THROUGH 11:

Without wetting the paint I started scribing the zimmerit pattern into the primer red areas using a sharp tool. After scribing the pattern I went over and chipped each of the primer red parts again using a stiff bristled paintbrush dampened with tap water. With this step I removed more of the primer red paint and subtly blended some of the scribed zimmerit pattern making it look more natural.

PHOTO 12:

Dark red-brown oils were blended over the primer red areas subtly blending the grey base with the different primer red tones.

PHOTO 13:

The final step was to add some very fine leftover amounts of zimmerit using a light tan Humbrol enamel paint. I used enamel instead of an acrylic because I needed the visible remnants of zimmerit to be very fine. If I over did this step I could quickly remove the paint using thinner. I used a calligraphy brush for this step. Good professional calligraphy brushes, although expensive, are great for chipping because they are designed to hold a lot of paint containing a very fine point.

PHOTO 14:

In photo 14 you can see the fine dark grey steel tones showing through where I scribed the zimmerit pattern into the coat of primer red.

You should know that I scribed through the dark grey down to the sand yellow base in a few areas. To fix this I simply went back over these areas with a fine brush using a grey acrylic paint. Also note the subtle various tones in the coat of primer red that resulted when I chipped the two different shades from the hairspray using a paint brush dampened with water. We can also see the fine light tan pattern of remaining zimmerit. These layers when coupled with the wet effects and earth tones display another example of how different techniques, or layers of effects, work together to give you a final authentic looking surface. Learning different techniques is only one thing. The important secret is understanding when and how to use combinations of these methods together that is the true secret to obtaining realistic finishes.

11 PAINTING EXTERIOR COMPONENTS & DETAILS

AFTER CHIPPING, AND PRIOR TO WEATHERING, IS A GOOD TIME TO PAINT SOME OF THE EXTERIOR DETAILS SUCH AS TOOLS, LIGHTS, EXHAUST PIPES AND TOW CABLES.

In fact there can be a rather large number of exterior components and stowage such as looted goods and sandbags depending on the subject. I usually wait until after the chipping to finish these details in order not to accidently get any paint on them when speckling rust for instance. Like all the other parts of a replica these details need considered attention. I also feel that they should, for the most part, be weathered with the rest of the model.

In this chapter I will cover the finishing of wooden handles, metal tools, spare track, lights, periscopes, exhaust pipes and rubber rimmed road wheels. These are all more of the common details that can add both life and colour to a model when painted correctly. We will start with painting wooden handles.

WOODEN HANDLES

WOODEN HANDLES ARE SMALL BUT IMPORTANT DETAILS.

Although sometimes a nuisance, the wooden handles of tools and other details will stand out nicely amongst all of the steel features seen on an AFV. As always you will need good bushes to paint these parts. Let's look at an example.

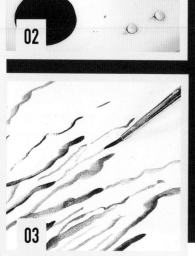

PHOTO 1:

In the case of this pick axe I started by painting the handle with a base coat of light tan acrylics mixed with a bit of yellow.

PHOTO 2 THROUGH 4:

Using Vallejo paints I diluted a red-brown tone with tap water. As with chipping, I wiped the excess paint away from the brush onto a piece of paper. Next I carefully painted the grain structure of the wooden handle.

PHOTO 5 AND 6:
Brown enamel filters were applied to the handle subtly blending the tan base coat and the grain structure.

PHOTO 7 THROUGH 10:
Dark brown artist oils where used to create shadows around where the handles are fastened finishing the detail. The gun cleaning rods on this Tiger II show another example of creating shadows in this manner. Highlighting the clamps also gives a more dramatic look to these details.

Both time and thought should be given to wooden details. Again, they really make nice looking details when painted well. Let's move forward with how to paint metal details such as tow cables and shovels.

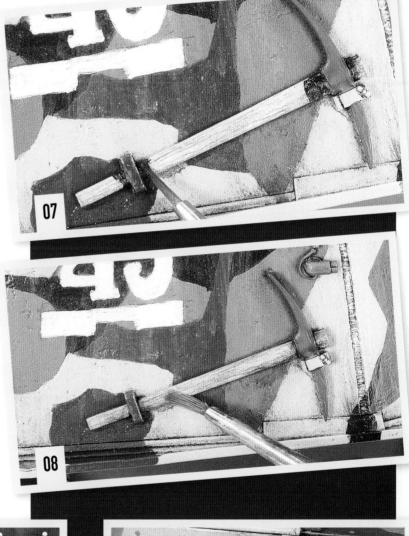

STEEL TOOLS AND DETAILS

FINISHING METAL TOOLS IS A RATHER SIMPLE TASK.

Many of the techniques have been discussed in the earlier chapters. Let's start with some tow cables.

PHOTO 1:
Tow cables are present on most AFVs. As a result of their purpose they are subject to a lot of wear and tear as seen on this example.

01

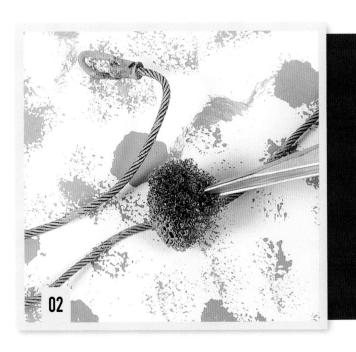

PHOTO 2 AND 3:
After applying a base coat to this T-34 cable both light green and brown chips were quickly applied using a sponge.

PHOTO 4:
Dark rust enamel washes were applied next.

PHOTO 5 AND 6:
More fine light green and rust chips where added using speckling.

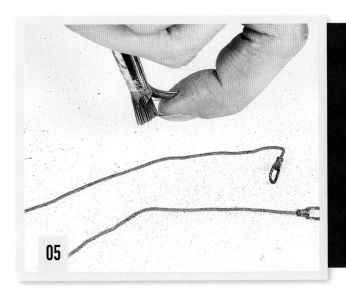

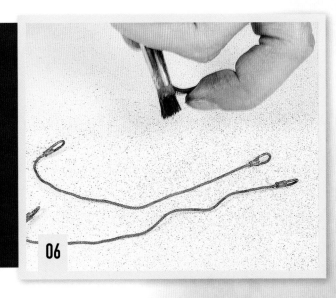

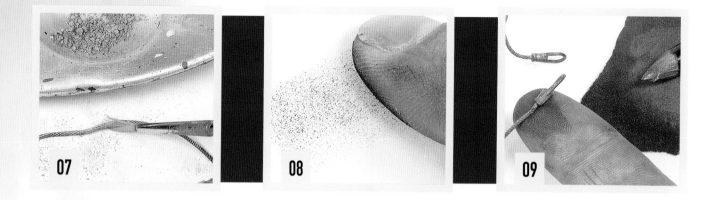

10

PHOTO 7 THROUGH 10:
After the wash had a day to dry pigments were randomly brushed on and blended using enamel thinner.

Graphite was lightly rubbed over the cable to add an realistic metallic shine to the chipping effects. First wipe the excess graphite from your finger onto a piece of paper to avoid getting

too much onto the part. We'll look further into using graphite to obtain authentic metal finishes later.

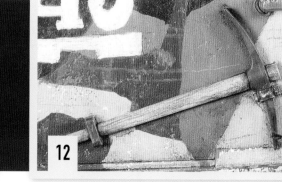

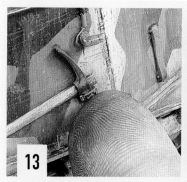

13

14

PHOTO 11 THROUGH 14:
I usually finish steel tools attached to the exteriors of armour models by first painting them with a grey tone mixed from acrylics. Next a random rust wash is applied. After the paint has had about a day to set graphite pigments are used to finish the details.

PHOTO 15 THROUGH 17:
Sometimes the tools are finished with the same tone as the base coat. Use effects like various amounts of chipping and rust to add contrast between the different parts such as on these gun cleaning rods.

15

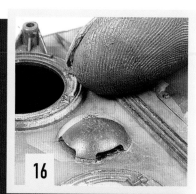

16

17

PAINTING SPARE TRACK

CREWS OF TANKS THROUGHOUT THE DIFFERENT CONFLICTS HAVE ALWAYS ADOPTED THE IDEA OF ATTACHING SPARE TRACKS ONTO THE SIDES OF THEIR VEHICLES TO SERVE AS EXTRA ARMOUR.

Spare tracks on replicas are always really cool looking details when finished nicely because they add character, texture and colour. Four different types are present on this Panzer IV ausf H giving a menacing appearance to the model. These tracks work in conjunction with the weathering, heavy paint chipping and damaged external components giving this replica a feeling of harsh days on the Russian front.

PHOTO 1 THROUGH 3:
The tones of rust on tracks can slightly vary depending on where it's manufactured and how long they have been outside. These examples photographed in Moscow, although old, show this clearly. Note the link with more of an orange hue in photo three. Altering rust tones on individual links as seen on the Panzer IV add both colour and realism to these details.

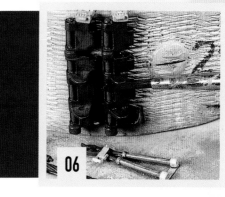

PHOTO 4 THROUGH 6:

It is always easier to paint details like spare track separate from the model.

In the case of this Tiger I needed to finish them attached to the turret. For these examples I mixed a dark brown base tone using acrylics. A very heavy dark rust wash mixed from enamels and pigments was randomly applied after the acrylics had about 15 minutes to set.

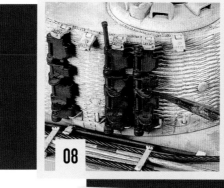

PHOTO 7 THROUGH 10:

I added some lighter rust pigments to the wash then applied it randomly such as into the corners of the teeth. Pigments were then brushed onto the specific areas in order to finish the details. Using dry pigments in this manner is great for blending different tones and effects.

It is simplest to weather these details with the rest of the vehicle. Remember that rusty surfaces are matt. Therefore these details will have always have dust stuck to them.

PHOTO 11 AND 12:

The spare track on the front of the JSU-152 were weathered separately allowing me more flexibility when applying the different effects. After adding a dark rust tone using an airbrush I employed a sponge to quickly add more different tones of rust flakes.

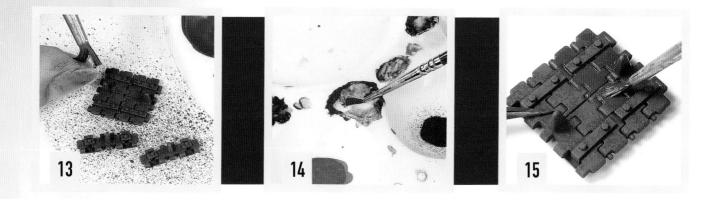

 PHOTO 13 THROUGH 15:
More rust effects and tones were applied with speckling. After letting the first layers of enamels set for a few hours some washes were added.

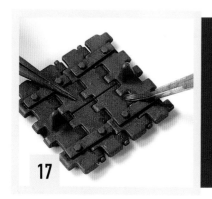
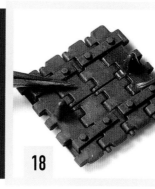

 PHOTO 17 THROUGH 19:
I mixed a lighter shade of rust again using enamels. I applied the light orange/brown tone to the right edge of each link then subtly blended it using thinner creating contrast between the parts. I let the track set for a few hours giving the enamels some time to dry. Next I applied some pin washes using a dark rust tone further distinguishing the links from one another.

PHOTO 20 THROUGH 23:
After some touch up using pigments graphite was used to finish the detail prior to weathering.

These two simple examples show how rust tones on tracks need to be built up in layers in order to obtain an authentic multi-toned oxidized appearance. More examples on creating various types of rusty surfaces will be demonstrated later.

21

22

23

PAINTING LIGHTS

PROPERLY PAINTING LIGHTS IS ESSENTIAL. UNREALISTIC LIGHTS CAN REALLY SUBTRACT FROM THE APPEARANCE OF A MODEL.

Lights are especially important on civilian vehicles such as this Hi-Lux as they are a major contributor to the overall appearance of the model. As with most other details there are after-market items available to make this task simpler. Painting lights is rather basic if you know the tricks. Let's look at a few examples.

PHOTO 1:

Tamiya has a number of glossy clear colors including the three primaries. These paints are good to have on hand for a number of tasks as you have already seen throughout this book. These paints along with a glossy silver enamel and fine brush are all that I usually use for finishing lights and reflectors.

PHOTO 2 AND 3:

Most of the new kits coming onto the market contain a sprue with clear parts such as periscopes and lenses for lights. For this Tamiya JSU-152 I painted the interior of the light housing using a silver enamel. After gluing the kit provided clear lens in place I gave it a wash of Tamiya smoke. The clear smoke adds shadows, brings out any detail on the lens and increases its glossy appearance.

01

02

03

PHOTO 4 AND 5:
I did not have a clear lens for the lights on this LVT. For this example I simply painted the exterior of the lens silver then added a filter of Tamiya smoke over it.

PHOTO 6:
The orange reflector on this M325 Nun-Nun Command car in use with the Lebanese army was painted in the same manner as the lights on the LVT. This time I simply used Tamiya Clear orange instead of smoke.

PERISCOPES

PERISCOPES ARE SOMETHING THAT WE ENCOUNTER ON JUST ABOUT ALL ARMOUR MODELLING SUBJECTS.

I seldom make open-topped vehicles therefore the periscopes that I paint are mostly hidden. Although this step-by-step is rather basic there are a few things that I would like to discus.

As I mentioned earlier, most armoured fighting vehicle kits now include clear sprues containing parts with glazed details such as lights and periscopes. As you know, the theory behind these transparent details is that they allow you to simply apply a liquid mask over the glazed areas, airbrush a coat of paint over the part, then remove the mask exposing the transparent smooth glossy surface underneath representing a layer of glass. The problem that I have encountered with this method on small parts such as 1/35th scale periscopes is that the coat of paint will sometimes flake or chip around the clear area when you remove the liquid mask resulting in a messy appearance.

There are also small masks on the market but they are not always available for the subject you are painting and sometimes difficult to come by. You can also cut small amounts of masking tape but this method can be a bit tedious especially if there are a lot of periscopes as often encountered in the cupolas of German subjects. I think that the easiest quickest way to represent small glazed surfaces on details like these is with a clear or gloss enamel. Here is a quick example.

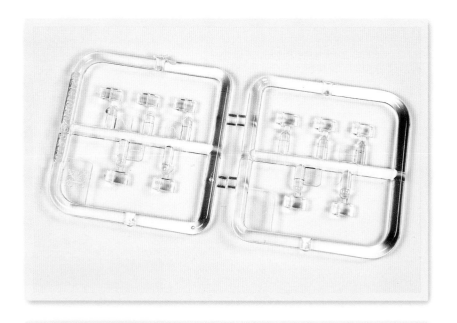

01

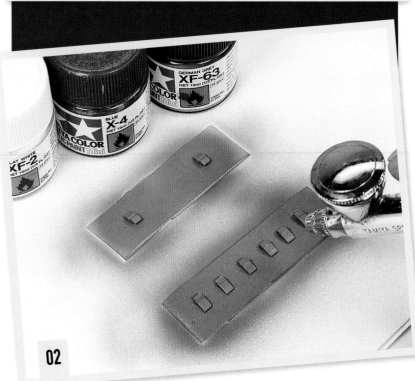

02

PHOTO 1 AND 2:
The first thing that I did was stick the small periscopes that needed to be painted for this E-50 onto a few pieces of tape. The rolled tape was stuck to a piece of paper for quick rotation during airbrushing. After letting the paint set the pieces were flipped over and reattached to the tape so I could quickly airbrush the opposite sides.

PHOTO 3 THROUGH 5:

Humbrol clear thinned to about one-part paint and one-part enamel thinner was then added using a small brush. Thinning the clear will help it to easily flow into all of the corners without much manipulation of the brush.

Painting small glazed surfaces in this manner is quick and easy. You can see on this E-50 that most of the periscopes are hidden within the cupola. The clear gloss representing the glass on these small details is sufficient.

PAINTING EXHAUST PIPES

LETS NOW LOOK AT PAINTING EXHAUST PIPES.

They involve techniques that we have discussed already. I recommend not gluing these parts to the model until you are ready to add the earth tones.

 PHOTO 1 THROUGH 3:
After airbrushing the entire piece with a very light grey containing a hint of red I created some dark rust chips using a sponge. Next I brushed on a thinned light blue toward the center. Remnants of the basecoat where added using a fine brush. Acrylics were used for these three steps.

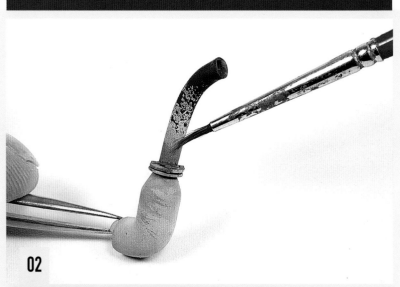

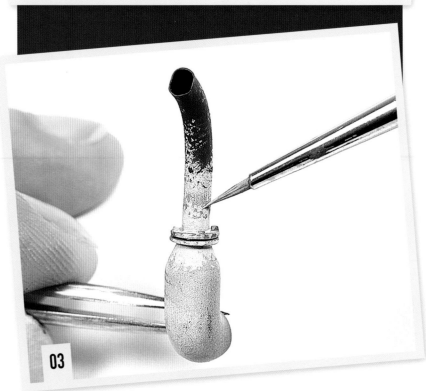

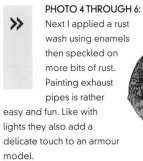

PHOTO 4 THROUGH 6:
Next I applied a rust wash using enamels then speckled on more bits of rust. Painting exhaust pipes is rather easy and fun. Like with lights they also add a delicate touch to an armour model.

06

PAINTING RUBBER ROAD WHEELS

PAINTING RUBBER ROAD WHEELS IS ONE OF THE FINAL TASKS THAT I PERFORM PRIOR TO WEATHERING.

I finish all of the other rubber details at this stage if there are any. If I were to paint these parts prior to chipping the grey finish would most likely be affected by the speckling effects. Painting these details can be rather dull especially when finishing a Tiger I containing 48 road wheels for example. For this short segment let's take a look at a few examples about how to finish road wheels with rubber exteriors.

I usually wait until the model is weathered to finish steel road wheels, drive sprockets and return rollers.

 PHOTO 1:

Sometimes, as in the case of this LVT, the wheels need to be glued in place prior to painting. With examples like this one you will need to be patient and carefully paint the rubber parts using a good fine brush. This LVT is a rare case as I never glue the wheels permanently to the model until the weathering is complete. Keeping these parts separate allow for easy access under the lower hull when applying earth tones and other effects.

01

 PHOTO 2:

There are masks and stencils to aid in the airbrushing of rubber rimed road wheels like this example from Quick Wheel. These products are available for most of the common kits on the market.

 PHOTO 3:

I always mix a light grey colour using approximately 1-part black and two-parts neutral grey as in this example when painting tires and most other rubber components.

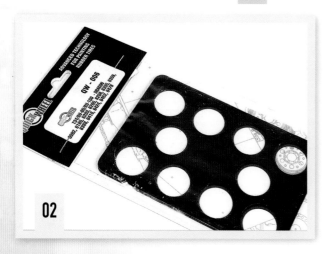

02

03

PHOTO 4 AND 5:
Rods such as toothpicks or old paint brushes work fine as handles allowing you to firmly hold the wheel keeping it steadily while carefully painting the sometimes narrow rubber exteriors. Painting the exterior of road wheels is tedious but it needs to be done.

This chapter covers most of the details encountered when painting an armour model. Now they will be able to be weathered along with the rest of the replica.

PAINTING MILD STEEL SURFACES AND RUST

RUSTY SURFACES ARE GREAT BECAUSE YOUR IMAGINATION IS THE LIMIT.

A good example is this Geschuzwagen Tiger Fur 17cm. Numerous types of different metal surfaces can be seen on this model. These different exteriors along with the fabricators markings and weathering really help to break the model apart giving each detail its own finish.

My interest for metal finishes comes from my early 20s when I was a welder. I really enjoyed working with steel until I decided to go back to finish my bachelors. In this part we are going to look at some examples for painting different mild steel finishes. You will find that most of the painting techniques used have been explained already. Therefore I will be less descriptive then I have been in the past chapters.

We will start with four examples for painting different types of surfaces on light guage metals.

PAINTING LIGHT GUAGE MILD STEEL AND SCREENS

WE ARE NOW GOING TO LOOK AT FOUR EXAMPLES OF PAINTING LIGHT GUAGE MILD STEEL.

The first example will require the use of a sponge as a primary technique to get a rusty finish. In the second example I will paint a screen assembly demonstrating how to use rust tones and other colors to make contrast between parts. For the third example we will paint a burnt piece of metal containing flaked paint. In the forth example the hairspray method will be employed to get a result representing a new piece of steel just taken from storage.

PAINTING SHEET METAL WITH A SPONGE

THE FOLLOWING SET OF STEP BY STEP PHOTOS DISPLAYS THE METHODS I USED TO PAINT AN OLD RUSTY PIECE OF SHEET METAL BEING USED AS A MAKE-SHIFT SCHÜRZEN ON A GERMAN E-50 'PAPER PANZER'

Most of the tones will be painted using layers of acrylic paints applied with a sponge. After I will slightly blend the colors while adding more tones using oils, enamels and pigments.

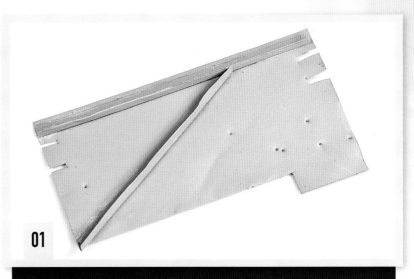

01

PHOTO 1 THROUGH 3:
After priming the part I airbrushed it with a bright rust basecoat mixed from acrylics. Next I mixed a few rust tones and some grey colors into the pools of a palette again using acrylics.

02

03

PHOTO 4 AND 5:

A base coat of grey was brushed over the two stiffeners. Next I brushed some of the light rust shade onto the corners of the angles.

PHOTO 6 THROUGH 8:

Using a sponge I added random darker brown tones over the orange rust. A paint brush was needed to apply more of the brown into the corners around the stiffeners where the sponge could not reach. More darker jumbled rust tones were applied using the same method.

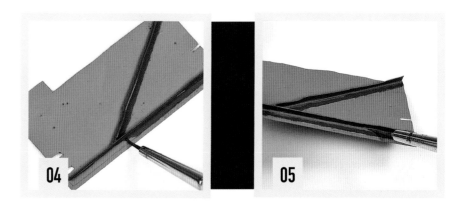

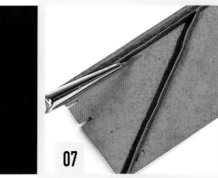

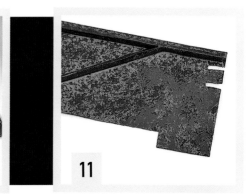

PHOTO 9 THROUGH 11:

I applied some random grey areas by brush representing left over bits of mill scale then added more bits or darker rust. These steps ended the layers of acrylics.

PHOTO 12 THROUGH 14:

Now it was time to add some additional tones while blending the acrylic layers using oils, enamel paints and pigments. The enamels were used to speed up the drying time of the oils. The pigments added extra colour and texture. Another orange rust tone was mixed, applied in dots, and then blended with the aid of enamel thinner. After I put the part down for about a day to let the oils set before moving on.

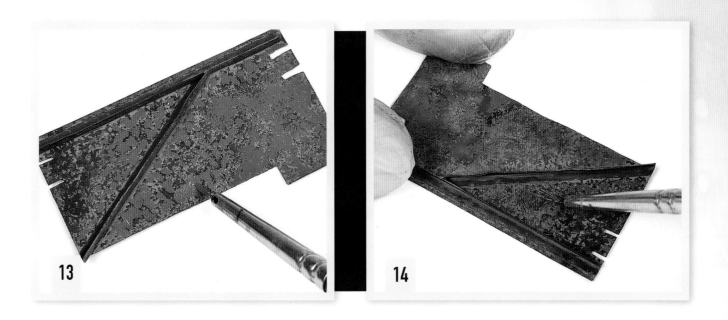

PHOTO 15 THROUGH 17:
Another darker rust shade was mixed, randomly applied in dots and blended like before. I applied some more rust tones over the angled stiffeners as well.

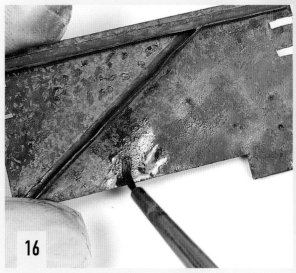

PHOTO 18 THROUGH 22:
More fine specs of the light and dark rust tones were applied by speckling. Some of the fine specs needed to be blended and cleaned from the areas of grey mill scale. I felt that a large rust streak would add a nice straight line to all of the jumbled tones. After that, I again put the part aside for a few days.

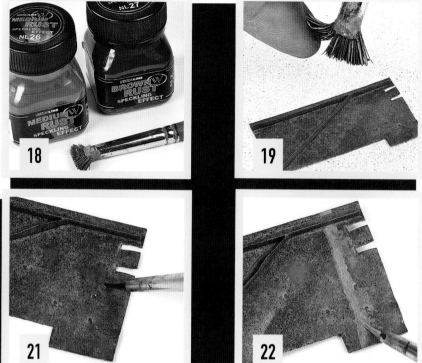

PHOTO 23 AND 24:
Next a few coats of matt varnish were added to the schürzen. A splash of spilt white paint was also applied to offset the orange streak of rust on the opposite side.

PHOTO 25 THROUGH 28:
I painted all of the small arms impacts using a fine brush then pressed a pencil into each of the small indents. Graphite was also rubbed over the angles and grey areas of mill scale using an artists sharpener. More shiny graphite was applied around the sides using my finger.

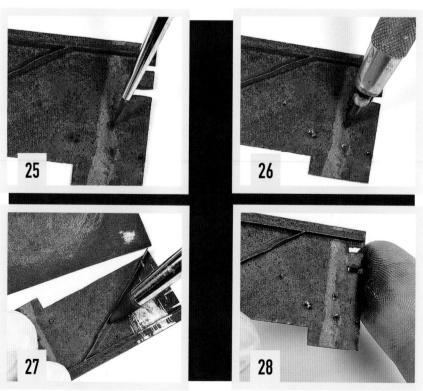

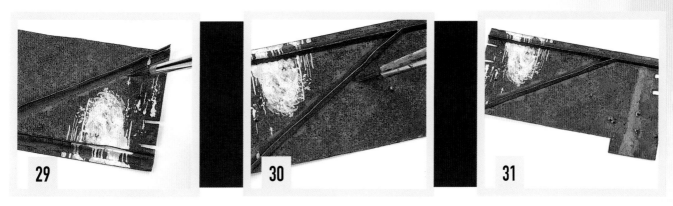

29

30

31

PHOTO 29 THROUGH 31:
I finished the schürzen by painting small rusty slag covered intermittent fillet welds around the angles.

This is an easy effective way for painting authentic rusty mild steel. You can use these same mediums and techniques to obtain an almost unlimited array of rusty metal surfaces on your model. Your imagination is the limit.

PHOTO 32 AND 33:
This steel pipe assembly is another example. I added all of the general tones using acrylics applied with both a sponge and paint brush. After random washes of enamels, oils and pigments where brushed on to add more tones while also blending everything together.

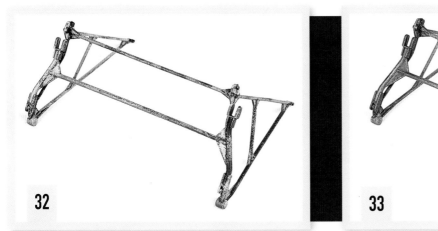

32

33

PAINTING METAL SCREENS

IN THIS QUICK EXAMPLE I WILL PAINT AN ANTI-PANZERFAUST SCREEN ASSEMBLY DEMONSTRATING HOW TO USE RUST TONES AND OTHER COLORS TO CREATE CONTRAST BETWEEN PARTS.

PHOTO 1 THROUGH 3:

After airbrushing a coat of primer a dark rust tone mixed from acrylics was applied. I mixed a medium rust tone using oils, enamels and pigments and applied a heavy coat over the entire screen assembly then added more rust tones using speckling.

PHOTO 4 AND 5:

After letting the medium rust tones dry for a while I painted grey areas of mill scale randomly over each of the different pieces of the frame.

PHOTO 6:

I brushed light enamel rust tones at the different intersections of the assembly creating contrast between the parts. Chipped light yellow areas of acrylic paint were added to some if the lengths using a sponge in order to break these pieces up from the rest of the structure. The white stripe was made using a sponge after masking the center area with tape.

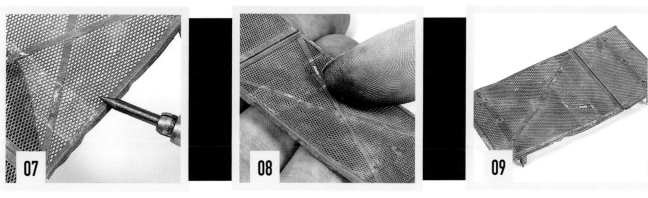

PHOTO 7 THROUGH 9:
Graphite was added using both a pencil and my finger to obtain random realistic shiny worn areas.

This is another method for painting mild steel and rust. Lets view another example this time on how to paint a burnt metal finish.

PAINTING BURNT SHEET METAL

FRESHLY BURNT SHEET METAL IS RATHER DISTINCTIVE HAVING A BRIGHT ORANGE RUSTY APPEARANCE.

I will continue with painting another one of the E-50 field applied schürzen this time to look as though it was taken from some burnt wreckage found in the field. In this example I am also going to apply a partial layer of peeled burnt paint. The bright orange rust along with the charred paint added two more textures to work in conjunction with the other mild steel patterns on the different schürzens helping to give a rather exotic look to this paper panzer. This series of steps will involve the hairspray technique discussed earlier.

PHOTO 1 THROUGH 3:
Metal leaf is a very thin delicate foil. There are different brands on the market and you can find it in most art stores. Wood glue diluted with water will be used in this example to fix the leaf onto the schürzen.

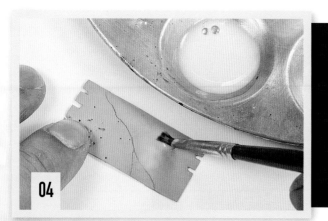

PHOTO 4 AND 5:
After priming my copper schürzen I roughly marked the area where the burnt paint would be. I brushed a thin layer of the diluted glue over the marked area then placed the schürzen face down onto a piece of the copper leaf. I let the parts sit for about six hours.

PHOTO 6 THROUGH 8:
I carefully cut the excess leaf away along with the unglued sections over the plate using a new sharp knife. I continued removing and peeling back the parts of remaining leaf until I obtainined a rough texture that I was happy with.

PHOTO 9 THROUGH 12:
A dry brush was used to remove any left over flakes. Diluted putty was used to blend the border between the copper foil and paint. After the putty had time to dry it was gently sanded.

PHOTO 13 THROUGH 18:
The base coat consisted of light and dark rust tones both mixed from the same three Tamiya paints. Starting with the burnt area I applied more light tones of rust using the speckling technique. Next I added more dark tones of rust again using speckling. Areas of grey mill scale were also added using a sponge.

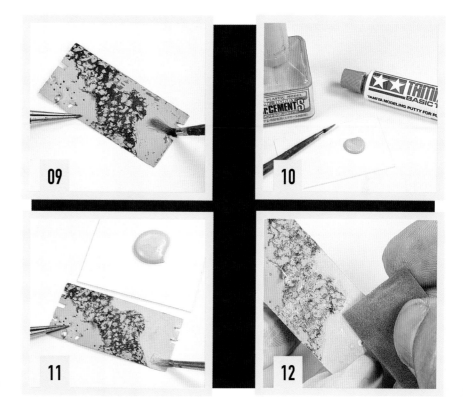

PHOTO 19 THROUGH 22:
I applied a coat of hairspray over the layers of acrylics. Next the dark grey and blue areas were airbrushed. The outer layer of hairspray and Tamiya paints were chipped using a small soft brush dampened with water. Once the water dried I sealed the paint with a few coats of matt varnish.

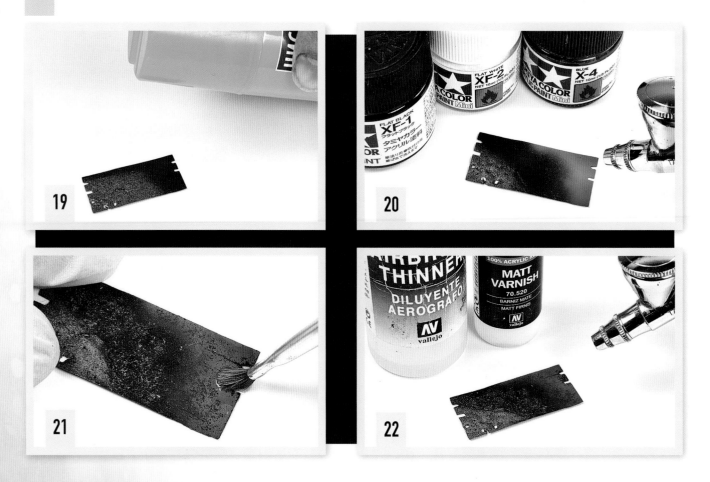

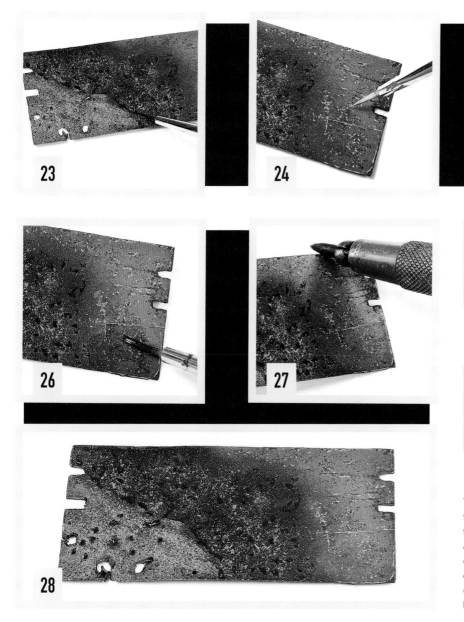

PHOTO 23 THROUGH 25:
I needed to paint some of the flakes black using a brush. I decided to apply some light blue chips to the blue paint. The impacts were also painted with a dark grey colour.

PHOTO 26 THROUGH 28:
Light amounts of rust washes were added to finish off the chipping effects. I traced the perimeter and impacts using a pencil to finish the part.

The bright burnt area of the steel and blistered flaked paint add more colour, texture and life to the completed E-50. Weathering parts like this is always difficult because you do not want to cover any of the layers needed to create the effects. Next we will look at a quicker example of painting a new piece of mild steel using the hairspray method.

PAINTING SHEET METAL, HAIRSPRAY TECHNIQUE

LIKE A SPONGE, USING HAIRSPRAY IS ALSO ANOTHER FAIRLY EASY METHOD THAT I USE FOR PAINTING MILD STEEL SURFACES.

For this example we are going to use the hairspray technique to paint the sheet metal assembly on the rear of this Sherman hull. Most of these techniques used will be a quick review of the ones covered earlier in this book.

» **PHOTO 1 THROUGH 3:**
After airbrushing a coat of primer I applied a basecoat of Tamiya German grey acrylic. Next a few good coats of hairspray were added. I airbrushed another light grey tone mixed from Tamiya paints. Using a scrubbing motion I removed some of the outer colour with a modified stiff-bristled brush dampened with water as shown.

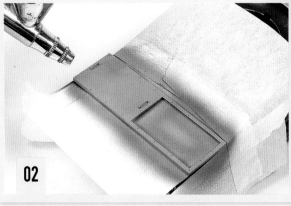

» **PHOTO 4 AND 5:**
At this point I airbrushed a few coats of matt varnish over the assembly sealing the light grey tone. After waiting for a few hours another few coats of hairspray were added. I mixed a rust colour using Tamiya paints, thinned the tone using water and then airbrushed it randomly over the part. Once more I removed some of the outer layer using a stiff-bristled modified brush as shown.

PHOTO 6 THROUGH 8:
» I outlined the edges of the frame using Humbrol aluminum. Graphite applied with my finger was used to tone down the aluminum coloured edges resulting in a look of worn steel.

This is the last example in this section about painting sheet metal. As you can see there are numerous ways to perform these types of finishes. Understanding all of them will help you to obtain many results adding lots of colors, textures and contrast amongst the different parts of a replica. Next I will demonstrate some methods for painting a thick piece of plate steel.

PAINTING STEEL PLATE

IN THIS PART I AM GOING TO PAINT A THICK STEEL PLATE LOCATED ON THE SIDE OF A JS-3 TANK WHERE THE SHEET METAL SIDE HAS BEEN RIPPED AWAY.

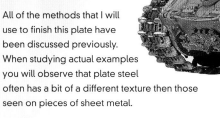

All of the methods that I will use to finish this plate have been discussed previously. When studying actual examples you will observe that plate steel often has a bit of a different texture then those seen on pieces of sheet metal.

 PHOTO 1 THROUGH 3:

For this example a brown tone mixed from acrylic paints was used for the base coat. Masking tape protected the rest of the dark green coat from overspray. Two to three coats of hairspray were applied next. A light grey mill scale tone mixed from acrylic paints was applied over the hairspray and randomly chipped using a fine brush dampened with tap water.

 PHOTO 4 AND 5:

Some random rust washes were applied then a light coat of orange rust was carefully airbrushed to the outer edge of the plate.

01

02

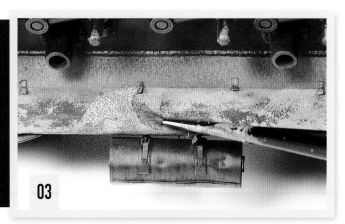

03

04

05

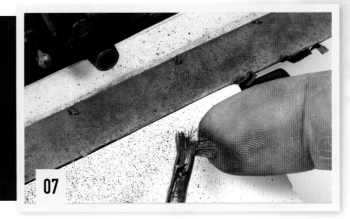

PHOTO 6 AND 7:
A brown rust tone was mixed and speckled onto the part to subtly blend all of the different layers.

PHOTO 8 AND 9:
Streaks of rust mixed from acrylic paints thinned with tap water were applied using a fine brush. An additional effect of green paint runs was also applied in the same manner to finish the part.

Although each of the colors and techniques used to paint the side plate of this JS-3 are very similar to methods seen earlier, thicker plates of steel often contain different textures. This Czech Hetzer in Prague during the uprising in 1945 demonstrates how numerous methods can be used to create an array of different surfaces on a scale model. These finishes are extremely enjoyable because they allow you to be very creative. I encourage you to try them on one of your future projects.

13 ADDING EARTH TONES AND EFFECTS

UP TO THIS CHAPTER WE HAVE COVERED METHODS FOR BOTH AIRBRUSHING AND BRUSH PAINTING FINISHES ALONG WITH ADDING VARNISHES, FILTERS, WASHES AND SHADOWS TO ENHANCE DETAILS.

Methods for creating authentic chipping effects and approaches to panting exterior components have also been presented. Having a good understanding on how to effectively finish each of these steps when painting a model will allow you to obtain a great base for applying the weathering effects covered in this next chapter. Although once controversial, the application of earth tones and weathering effects to scale models has become more accepted over the past decade. Applying these effects gives the modeller another level of creativity. If done properly the weathering effects used with the other techniques described throughout this book can give you a very realistic model that you will enjoy looking at on your shelf time and time again. Sometimes I will choose a subject simply for its weathering potential such as the case of the LVT seen throughout the pages of this book. In fact, I really have no interest in the LVT at

all. I just knew that this subject would give me an opportunity to apply some thick, wet, runny mud in a way that I have not had the opportunity to do on other replicas.

There are now many techniques and products available for adding weathering effects that are being used by modellers. Of course not all of them are necessary for finishing every model. There are some methods that I have yet to try and they all take practice. You will see that all of the weathering methods covered in the following descriptions are applied in layers, and,

as I said earlier, work best in conjunction with other finishing techniques.

During this chapter we are going to discuss the following:
- Examples for Applying Rainmarks and Dust
- Mud Spatters
- Weathering Tracks and Running Gear
- Heavy Dust and Thick Layers of Mud

I strongly recommend first referencing photos of weathered vehicles to familiarize yourself with how different weathering effects look. Google

Image search is great tool for finding such pictures. Visiting local construction sites is another option although I have found that the equipment operators often get uneasy when people start photographing them.

If you are going to weather a Sherman tank for example, do not only limit yourself to photos of M4s. The effects seen on most AFVs will help to give you ideas. With all of this in mind let's move forward with examples for applying rainmarks and dust. These effects will work as the base for all of the subsequent weathering steps needed to complete a model.

APPLYING DUST AND RAINMARKS

APPLYING DUST AND RAINMARKS IS USUALLY THE FIRST AND MOST IMPORTANT WEATHERING STEP.

Random layers of dust and rainmarks will serve as both a base and guide for a lot of the subsequent effects such as thicker layers of mud grease and even exhaust stains.

Rainmarks represent faint vertical lines of dust that have been washed downward by rainfall. This is why the effect is referred to as "Rainmarks".

Dust and rainmarks can be rather subtle as seen on the upper surfaces of this JS-3. Although sometimes faint, these matt effects contrast nicely with the model's satin basecoat as discussed at the beginning of this book. Rainmarks and dust effects can also help you to create contrast between details such as on the hull sides and large upper plates of this Geschutzwagen Tiger II .

On this T-34 we see another example of using dust tones to help create contrast. You can see how the transmission cover sticks out from the rest of the upper hull as a result of the dust along with other effects such as grease and colour modulation. These effects are all working together to emphasize this fragile detail while also breaking up the rear hull making the replica more lively.

During this segment I am going to discuss four examples for applying these sometimes faint but important effects. Like with washes and filters you will see that the results you obtain with rainmarks and dust will differ between satin and matt surfaces. I will also show an example of applying rainmarks and dust over colour modulation. Throughout these different cases

you will notice that wet effects also play an important role in enhancing rainmarks and dust effects. Let's now look at a simple example over a more common satin surface.

APPLYING DUST AND RAINMARKS OVER A SATIN SURFACE

OUR FIRST EXAMPLE FOR APPLYING RAINMARKS AND DUST WILL BE OVER A SATIN SURFACE THAT WE COMMONLY WEATHER WHEN PAINTING A VEHICLE.

For ease of demonstration I decided to use a piece of sheet plastic for this first example. I think this is the simplest way to demonstrate how I use this method in layers to accomplish the overall effect.

PHOTO 1 AND 2:
The first step that I perform when creating rainmarks is to apply a light random grey-tan coat over the subject using Tamiya acrylics.

01

02

PHOTO 3 AND 4:
To continue this step you are going to need a few fine brushes. Any fine pointed low-end brush will work for this technique. The second step also involves acrylic colors. I took a palette and filled two of the pools with water. I mixed a another light grey-tan colour using a brush to add fine amounts of the paint at a time until obtaining another tone a bit darker than the one airbrushed before. You will want your dust colour to contain about one part paint and ten parts water.

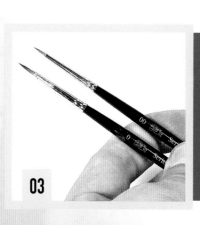

03

04

PHOTO 5 THROUGH 9:

If the surface that you are applying the rainmarks to is small or narrow, as in this case, I would recommend first wiping some of the mix from your brush onto a dinner napkin. Start applying the watery mix over the surface using vertical strokes as shown, let it dry, and then repeat the process. Photo eight shows the part after the third pass of applying the watery mix. Note how faint rainmarks are starting build up becoming more evident. Photo nine shows that surface after four layers of the mix.

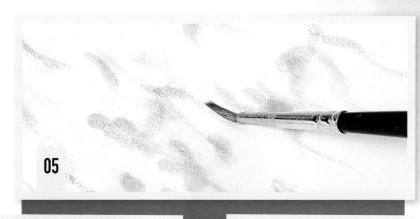

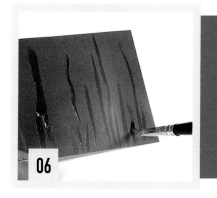

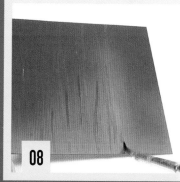

TRY TO KEEP IN MIND THE FOLLOWING:

It is very important to remember a few things. You will see that the watery mix of dust will start to bead up at first on satin surfaces. This is perfectly fine. This same effect happens on all satin surfaces of actual vehicles. Faint spots of the matt dust tone are evident on the upper sides of the E-75 turret and hull seen in these books. After three to four passes you will start to build up a matt surface making it easier to create fine vertical streaks.

PHOTO 10 AND 11:

Moving on I continued applying more vertical streaks. Photo ten contains around eight or nine passes. Note how I am now focusing the vertical strokes more on the dust pattern airbrushed before. As your rainmarks become more evident start using the random airbrushed coats of dust as your guide. In photo 11 I also began focusing more on the lower areas supposedly closer to the ground when applying the final passes.

ADDING EARTH TONES AND EFFECTS   **160**

PHOTO 12:

Photo 12 shows the square with the rainmarks completed. I enjoy applying rainmarks in this manner. This method allows me to build them up slowly until getting a result which I am happy with. The XF series of Tamiya paints are very matt allowing for nice flat layers of rainmarks and dust that contrast nicely with the satin basecoat making the model more authentic looking.

PHOTO 13 AND 14:

You can brush on dry pigments to touch up areas in the rain marks that you are not happy with. After you can apply more vertical strokes using enamel thinner to blend and fix the pigments if you like.

PHOTO 15 THROUGH 18:

Glossy areas, often referred to as "Wet Effects" can really enhance rainmarks. I created more random lines and shapes using a thinned enamel gloss. You can also buy pre-mixed wet effects from a number of different brands.

Next I subtly combined the wet vertical lines and shapes with more thinned gloss enamel, this time using the speckling technique. I masked the upper part of the square using paper. In this case I wanted to place more of the specs on the lower area. Again, dry pigments were lightly brushed on to blend some of the glossy areas.

PHOTO 19 AND 20:

On the completed part you can see that the matt rainmarks create a very genuine coat of dust over a satin surface. The wet areas also add to the authentically breaking up the matt dust tones. This is a great example of how some effects work much better together then when just applied alone. The KV-2X walker is an example of a model that was weathered using only the dust and rainmark techniques demonstrated in this segment. Again note how the wet effects play a vital role in adding both authentically and character to this menacing looking model. I am sure that you can use other thinned acrylics such as Vallejo and Life Colour for creating rainmarks. I have always used Tamiya paints for these effects because I am familiar with the matt properties of this brand. I will create more rainmarks in some upcoming examples using enamels and gouache paints.

APPLYING DUST AND RAINMARKS OVER A MATT SURFACE

WITH THE ABUNDANT CHOICE OF DIFFERENT SUBJECTS NOW AVAILABLE AS PLASTIC KITS, THEORETICAL AFVS THAT NEVER GOT PAST THE DESIGN STAGES, REFERRED TO AS PAPER PANZERS, AND OTHER EXOTIC PROTOTYPES HAVE BECOME MORE POPULAR.

These themes give the modeller an opportunity to be more creative with the finish. Some of the popular choices for painting paper panzers are matt finishes like factory applied primer red and unpainted steel. Rainmarks and dust effects tend to act a bit differently when applied onto a matt surface. Although most of the techniques in this part will be a review of what we've just covered there are a few things that I want to demonstrate.

PHOTO 1 AND 2:
As in the previous example I started by airbrushing a random coat of dust focusing on the lower areas of the part. As a result of the matt surface you will see that it is much easier to create subtle vertical streaks of rainmarks. In photo two you are seeing the effects after only the second layer of vertical passes. If your mix has too much paint you will quickly obtain opaque unnatural looking rainmarks. This is because the pigments in the wash will adhere quickly to the rough microscopic texture of the matt surface. Therefore, I would recommend trying your mix on a matt test piece to make sure that your water-paint ratio is to your liking before performing this process on the model.

PHOTO 3 AND 4:
Pigments also adhere much better to matt surfaces so be very conservative applying them only in small amounts at a time. Once the pigments are brushed onto a matt surface they are pretty much there to stay. You will be able to blend them a little with enamel thinner.

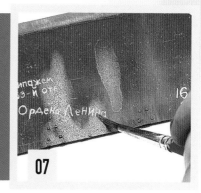

05 **06** **07**

PHOTO 5 THROUGH 7:

This time I made a damp earth tone using a Humbrol enamel mixed with some dirt coloured pigments creating variations in the rainmarks and dust effects. Some enamel gloss was also added to the blend. I applied the enamel mix in random areas and blended it with thinner. We will talk more about using damp and wet earth tones in the upcoming sections.

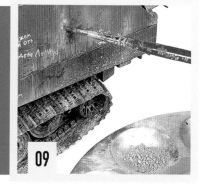

08 **09**

PHOTO 8 AND 9:

As with rainmarks, wet effects will also be much more evident on a matt surface if you do not first thin the gloss. This is because the glossy appearance of this effect will contrast more with a matt facade than with a satin one like in the previous example. Once again you can

carefully brush on dry pigments to subtly blend these effects to your liking.

Rainmarks and pigment applications act differently on matt surfaces. If your paint to water ratio is right you will find rainmark application to actually be easier and rather enjoyable over a matt surface. Again, I need to stress that you

apply the pigments in light amounts at a time. Once pigments are placed onto a matt surface it is almost imposible to remove or even blend them. One method for reducing areas where you feel the dust application to be too strong is to carefully airbrush some faint amounts of the basecoat back over these parts.

APPLYING DUST AND RAINMARKS OVER COLOUR MODULATION

IN THIS SEGMENT I WILL DEMONSTRATE THE APPLICATION OF DUST TONES AND RAINMARKS ONTO A MODEL CONTAINING COLOR MODULATION.

Although applying these techniques are the same as explained previously, different dust tones will be needed over the various shades and gradients.

In this case you will see that I started by airbrushing two different shades of dust. A dark tone was used for the recessed shaded areas and a lighter one for the other surfaces. Three different shades of rainmarks were then mixed although two will usually work fine depending on how dramatic the colour modulation is. Four tones of pigments were used over the light and dark areas while also adding variations in the layers of dust. In this example we will be continuing with the LVT as it was left after application of the chipping effects discussed earlier.

01

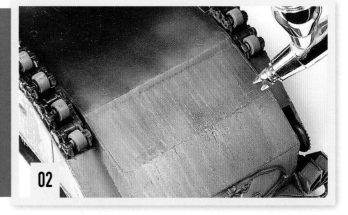

02

PHOTO 1 AND 2:
I started by airbrushing a rather dark random tone of dust mixed from Tamiya paints. I focused this dark shade into all of the recessed areas where shadows would be. These places included under the fenders, onto the lower parts of the hull and around the upper hull where the turret would sit.

PHOTO 3 AND 4:
Next a lighter dust tone was also applied in arbitrary amounts over the upper hull. Light streaks were airbrushed onto the sides where large amounts of mud were going to be dripping down. I also applied some lighter random coats of dust to the outer parts of the lower hull under the model.

03

04

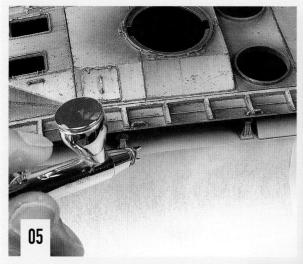

PHOTO 5 THROUGH 7:
Thick deposits of mud would be present on the horizontal plane below the fenders as a result of the returning track. Tape was used to mask the sides of the vehicle. Although a rather heavy layer of earth would be present over these surfaces I wanted to keep the dust on the upper sides lighter and more random.

PHOTO 8:
For the rain marks I mixed three earth tones each containing a mix of about one part acrylic paint and ten parts water.

PHOTO 9:
I used the random airbrushed layers of matt dust as my guide for the rainmarks during this step. Although I had a dark tone, the medium shade was the predominant colour used. The lighter colour was applied where the rainmarks were the heaviest for added tones in these areas. You can see that the medium tone was used in the darker recessed areas to give more tones to these shady areas. I would urge caution as the light grey colour can appear almost white in these darker parts.

PHOTO 10 THROUGH 12:
The watery mix of rainmarks was applied to the horizontal surfaces with a larger round brush using a circular motion. It is best to keep tapping the diluted mix until it is fairly dry. You can use a hairdryer to speed up the drying process during this step. Photos 11 and 12 show the LVT with the dust tones and rainmarks completed. As I said earlier, the advantage of adding earth tones in this manner is that you can subtly build up the dust and rainmarks to a point where you feel they look convincing. See how the rainmarks will help to give more of a realistic muddled appearance to the faint layers of dust airbrushed on in the previous step.

PHOTO 13 THROUGH 15:
I mixed four pigment tones to add more earth shades while also subtly blending the rainmarks as seen when comparing photos 14 and 15.

15

PHOTO 16:
Pigments were also applied to the horizontal surfaces and blended with enamel thinner to add further tones to the dust.

PHOTO 17:
The techniques needed for applying dust and rainmarks to a surface with colour modulation are no different than those discussed earlier. More tones in the airbrushed layers of dust, rainmarks and pigments are often necessary depending how dramatic your colour modulation is. Now this model has a good base for the heavier weathering and wet effects that will be discussed and applied later.

16

17

APPLYING DUST TONES AND RAIN MARKS USING GOUACHE PAINTS

OVER THE PAST FEW YEARS I HAVE BEEN INCREASINGLY USING GOUACHE PAINTS AS A MEANS FOR WEATHERING MODELS.

Gouache paints are an opaque water-soluble paint. Like water colors they have a bonding agent but contain more pigments making them thicker, very matt and more opaque. They tend to dry to a lighter tone then what you will observe when they are still wet so some practice is needed when mixing them.

Gouache paints have certain properties making them ideal for weathering. They dry very matt making them good for creating earth and rust colors. The biggest advantage is that you can apply gouache paints and blend them further with water after they have dried as I will demonstrate. As Gouache is water-soluble you can apply subsequent finishing effects over them using enamel paints.

Like all other mediums some practice is needed to effectively use gouache paints. Like most other methods gouache paints will give you the best results when used with other finishing techniques. Therefore this chapter will contain some finishing steps discussed previously.

 PHOTO 1 THROUGH 5:
I started by airbrushing an earth tone using acrylic paints onto the lower hull and randomly over the upper parts and super structure. This random coat will act as a base for the upcoming dust tones and rain marks. As always I airbrushed thin amounts of dust around various details such as the hatches creating contrast. A piece of paper was used to mask details such as the tools keeping these objects clean distinguishing them from the rest of the superstructure.

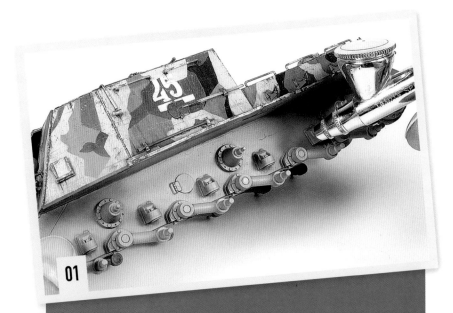

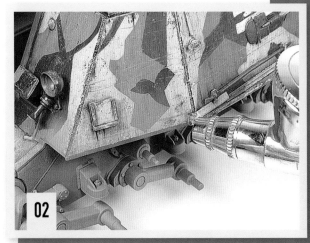

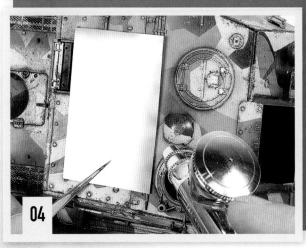

PHOTO 6 AND 7:
The drive sprockets, return rollers, road wheels and idler wheels also received a random coat of dust. Make sure this coat is transparent keeping the chipping effects evident as shown.

PHOTO 8 THROUGH 11:
When working with gouache paints it is best to place a small amount onto an aluminum palette with some water. You will find that you need to thin them differently depending on the application. In the case of rainmarks you should dilute some of the paint using the tap water as shown, wipe the excess away onto a piece of paper, and then apply vertical fine streaks onto the side of the model using a small brush. Focus more of the random length streaks toward the lower areas of the superstructure as shown.

Practice on a piece of painted scrap plastic to become familiar with the properties of Gouache prior to applying them to your model. They are another type of paint containing their own characteristics that you should first familiarize yourself with.

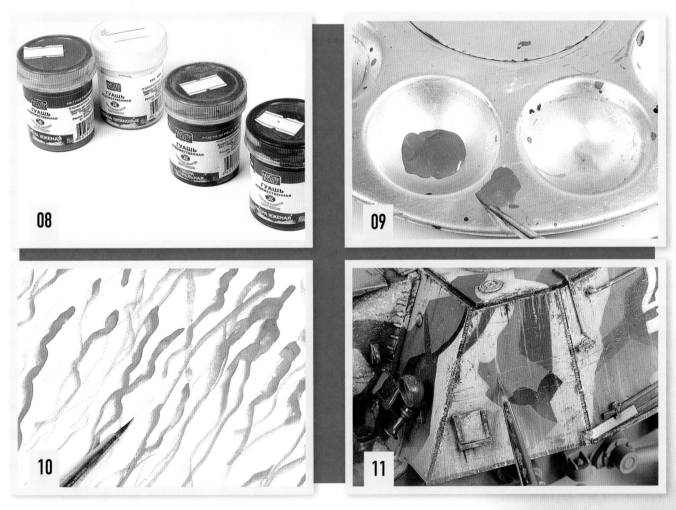

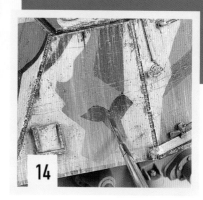

 PHOTO 12 THROUGH 14:
Next blend the fine lines using the same brush dampened with only water. If you are not happy with the appearance of the rainmarks you can add some more fine lines and blend them.

 PHOTO 15 AND 16:
You can see that gouache can be an effective means of adding subtle rainmarks onto the surface of a replica. Gouache is also more forgiving than acrylic paints for this application in that you can soften and continue to work them using water after they have dried.

PHOTO 17 THROUGH 20:

Adding layers of dust with gouache paints is easy. After thinning the paint with water I brushed a layer onto the fenders. Once it had some time to dry I softened the paint using water and removed much of it from the inner parts as shown in photo 20. Observe the resulting muddled appearance of the earth tone. Keeping the stiffeners on the outer edges of the fenders clean will help to create contrast between these details and the rest of the dusty fender.

PHOTO 21 AND 22:

On the front rounded fender I blended the gouache paints downward using a small damp brush creating rainmarks.

PHOTO 23 AND 24:

Dust was also blended in the same manner around other details on the model. I did this by by first brushing on the gouache dust coloured paints into the corners then blending them outward using tap water. Note how this step works in conjunction with the acrylic dust tones airbrushed earlier creating an realistic random layer of dust.

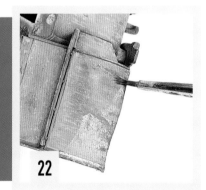

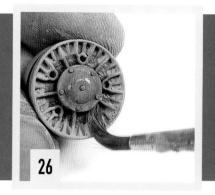

PHOTO 25 THROUGH 27:
I coat of mud was also placed around the outer diameter of the wheels and blended.

PHOTO 28:
Moving toward the lower part of the hull, heavier amounts of earth were applied. There are a few ways to create thick mud as I will also demonstrate later on. In this example I created thick amounts of dry earth using a mixture of gauche paints, plaster and sifted sand. I applied this mixture onto the lower and rear parts of the hull using speckling.

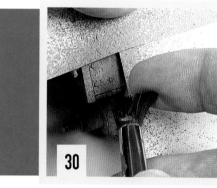

PHOTO 29 THROUGH 31:
Mud splashes usually stay more toward the lower parts of the hull. Pieces of paper were used to keep any specks of paint from getting on the upper parts. Pieces of paper where also used to keep the speckling confined toward the rear of the hull over the tracks. The dry mud mixture was also speckled over the running gear.

PHOTO 32:
I applied more if the gouache mud mix onto the lower hull and blended it downward again using water to create runs.

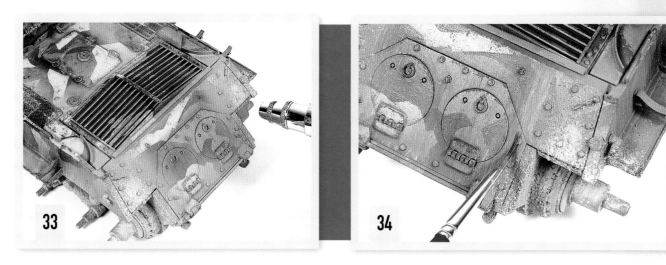

PHOTO 33 AND 34:
After the speckling I felt that the thick layers of mud did not look natural on the rear of the hull above the tracks. I airbrushed some more dust using acrylic paints. More rainmarks were blended using gouache. You will often need to go back and forth between techniques on certain parts of a model in order to get a result that you feel is natural in appearance.

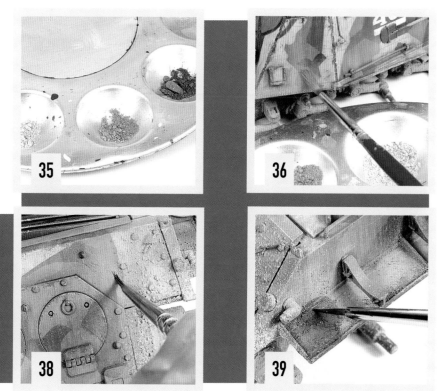

PHOTO 35 THROUGH 39:
One of the final steps in applying the dust was to bush on a few different coloured dry pigments over some of the gouache rainmarks subtly blending any areas that I felt to be unnatural in appearance. Thinner was used on the rear plate to further blend the pigments in these heavily weathered areas. Note that the enamel thinner will not influence the water-based gouache paints applied earlier.

PHOTO 40:
You can use darker pigments to create shadows underneath details such as this mantlet cover.

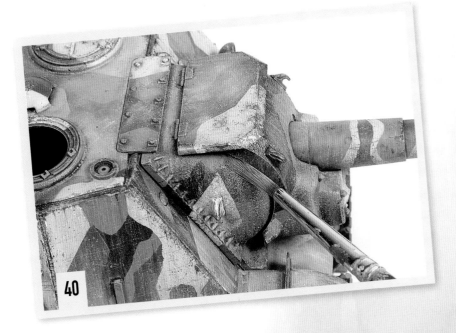

PHOTO 41 THROUGH 44:
Darker, damper earth tones will add both colour and texture to a weathered replica as seen on the running gear of this T-55 engineering vehicle. I mixed a dark earth tone using Humbrol enamels, gloss varnish and some earth coloured pigments for added texture. Starting with the running gear I applied the dark earth mix onto the wheels using a brush and then blended the tone using turpentine.

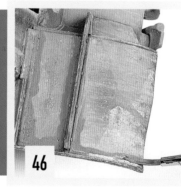

PHOTO 45 THROUGH 47:
Damp earth effects will also help to create further contrast between details.

PHOTO 48:
The damp earth tone was also speckled over some of the areas where large amounts of mud would build up.

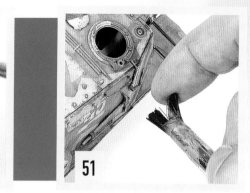

49 **50** **51**

PHOTO 49 THROUGH 51:

The final step was to apply some wet effects to the hull and running gear for yet more texture. As I have said in earlier segments, adding glossy wet areas is a great and easy way to break up rainmarks making the coats of dust more authentic. Subtle thinned amounts of gloss were also speckled over the model to further break up the dust tones while subtly unifying the larger damp areas.

52

PHOTO 52:

Tamiya clear is also a great medium for adding glossy effects such as the wet areas in the grooves of this Tiger II wheel. In this case I simply painted the clear right over the damp earth effects.

Gouache is another option for adding dust tones and rainmarks onto a model. These paints are more flexible because they can be reworked with a wet paintbrush. Gouache is very opaque so you will need to thin them prior to using this medium for applying rainmarks.

Appling dust tones and rainmarks are usually the first and most important weathering step. You will see the techniques covered in this chapter will now work as both a base and guide for the upcoming weathering steps and effects needed to realistically finish an armour model and most other types of replicas. In the next segment we will continue with more examples for applying mud spatters. Applying different mud spatters also plays an important role in obtaining an good weathered finish.

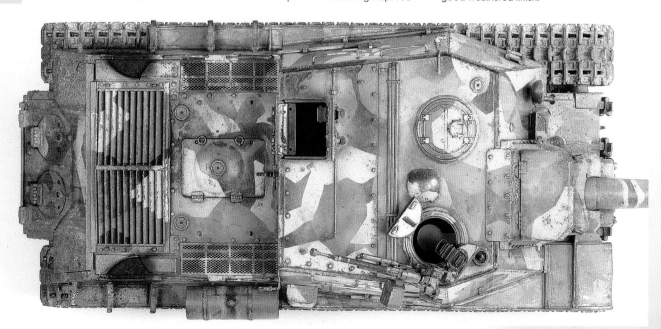

EARTH SPATTERS

ALTHOUGH I PREVIOUSLY DEMONSTRATED THE EFFECTIVENESS OF EARTH SPATTERS USING GOUACHE PAINTS I WOULD ALSO LIKE TO TALK ABOUT THIS IMPORTANT TECHNIQUE IN MORE DETAIL USING TAMIYA PAINTS.

I use the steps shown in this short section on every armour model that I finish. You can use earth spatters throughout different stages of the weathering process. This technique will help add to the authentic appearance to your dust tones and rainmarks. Earth spatters will also give a very natural look to areas containing heavy amounts of mud. Applying mud spatters is accomplished best with the speckling technique. Let's look at a few examples.

PHOTO 1 THROUGH 6:
The earth spatter mix that we will use in these examples is a concoction of four different ingredients. What I did in this case was to use a spare jar to keep the mixture stored for use on future models. After mixing a light dust tone with Tamiya paints I added some Plaster of Paris and sifted sand then mixed everything together. The mix that I usually make contains about four parts paint, two parts plaster and 1 part sifted sand. A little water is sometimes needed to soften the mixture. The results that you are looking for will differ depending on the proportions that you add of each ingredient.

PHOTO 7 THROUGH 11:

Take a bit of the mix and place it onto a palette. Thin the mix by adding some more water with a stiff bristled brush. With the same stiff bristled brush use the speckling technique to very carefully apply the earth coloured mix onto different parts of the model. Paper can be used to mask details during this step. Photo 10 shows the side of the hull after lightly applying the earth spatters. After the mix dries you can take a dry clean brush and carefully sweep away the excess amounts of the mix obtaining a subtle random effect faintly visible in photo 11.

PHOTO 12 THROUGH 14:

In photos 12 through 14 you can see another example of applying the earth spatters with the aid of paper masks in order to keep the effects refined to specific areas. In this case I continued to let the dust tones and rainmarks guide the application of this earth effect as recommended previously in the section on rainmarks.

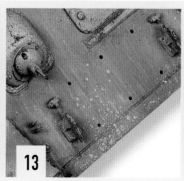

PHOTO 15 THROUGH 17:
Here is one more example of using paper to mask the application of earth spatters onto the lower hull sides of this Geschuzwagen Tiger Fur 17cm.

PHOTO 18 THROUGH 22:
I always apply heavier layers onto the running gear. I usually start by lightly applying the earth mix using a brush to place it onto the outer areas of the wheel. Next I apply more of the mix using speckling. Let the mix dry for an hour and then carefully remove some (but not all) of the effect using a stiff brush. You can also use a toothpick to eliminate some of the larger more rigid chunks.

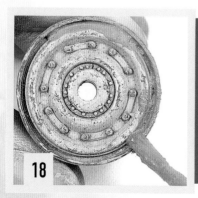

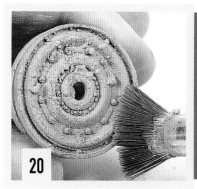 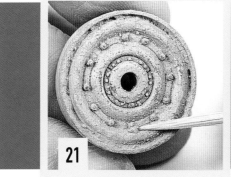 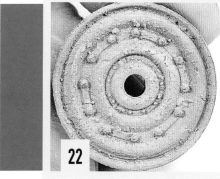

PHOTO 23:
Photo 23 shows the weathered wheel on the completed model. As with all techniques, earth spatters should be used in conjunction with other weathering effects such as darker earth tones, wet areas and grease stains.

Earth spatters using Tamiya paints, plaster and sifted sand will add another rather subtle layer to your dust tones and rainmarks making your finish more lifelike. You will see this mix used throughout the next chapter as a step in finishing tacks and applying heavy earth tones.

23

WEATHERING TRACKS

UNTIL RECENTLY THE TRACKS AND RUNNING GEAR ARE OFTEN NEGLECTED IN COMPARISON TO THE REST OF THE MODEL IN REGARDS TO PAINTING AND WEATHERING.

As I said in the first of these two books tracks and running gear often cover roughly one third of the model's exterior. Tracks are also one of the details that make AFVs so interesting. Therefore it is vital that they are finished in layers using the same techniques as on the rest of the model.

This part will cover the types of track assembled in the first book. An example using the flexible kit provided rubber band type will also be included. The techniques discussed in the four following examples can be used on most other types of track sets available. Let's get started with the injection molded plastic individual linked types often included in the plastic kits.

WEATHERING GLUEABLE PLASTIC TRACKS

IN THIS SEGMENT I WILL BE CONTINUING WITH THE SECTIONS OF JSU-152 TRACK ASSEMBLED DURING THE FIRST BOOK.

These tracks will be painted with some of the same techniques in a similar order as demonstrated on the JSU-152 in the chapter entitled, "Applying dust tones and rain marks using gouache paints". Remember to keep the runs of links for the right and left sides of the model separate from each other. If you mix them up the sags on the tracks over the return rollers may not align properly.

» **PHOTO 1:**
For this example I will start by airbrushing the track with three good coats using an acrylic matt brown paint. Tape the tracks onto a piece of paper to keep the sections from blowing away while you are airbrushing them. Rotate the paper between each coat in order to properly get the paint into all of the corners of these complex details.

» **PHOTO 2 AND 3:**
A dry earth tone of gouache was brushed over the outer parts of the track. I used my finger to rub away the wet paint from the outer edges keeping these areas smooth for the metallic effects that would be added later.

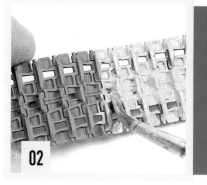

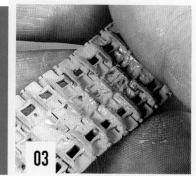

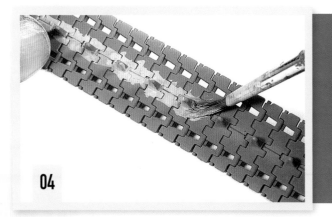

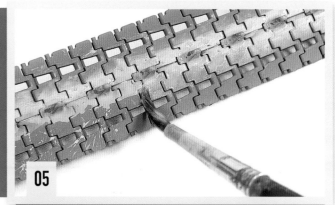

» **PHOTO 4 THROUGH 6:**
The dry earth tone of gouache paint was then applied to the inner parts of each section and blended with a wet brush. I also applied the earth tone to the outer edges then blended it in the same manner

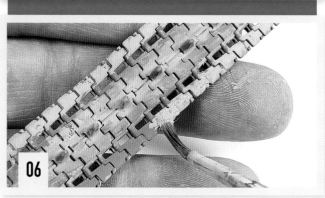

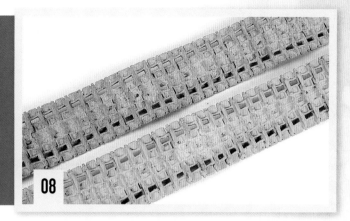

PHOTO 7 AND 8:
I added some grey to the dry earth gouache and applied this darker tone to the outer and inner sections of the track using the speckling technique. This darker tone will add more earth shades to the tracks. This is evident in photo eight on the upper run when compared to the length below it with a single dry earth tone.

PHOTO 9 THROUGH 15:
I made a mix using Humbrol brown with pigments and enamel gloss to represent a damp mud tone. After applying this mix I blended it using enamel thinner. I also added some damp earth to some of the individual links on the inner sides of the treads to break up the dry earth tones. More of the damp earth was speckled onto both the outer and inner parts of the runs as shown.

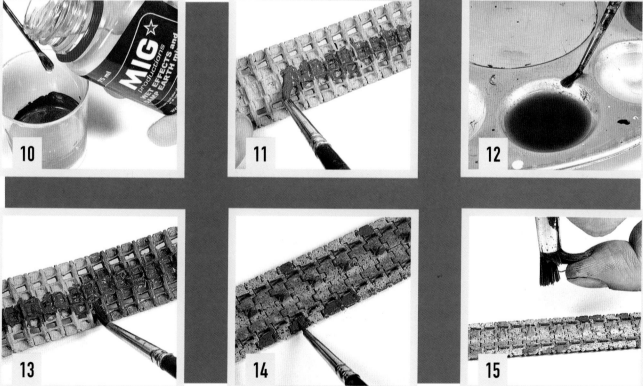

PHOTO 16:
Tamiya clear straight from the bottle works great for adding glossy wet looking eras over effects such as earth tones. After this step the tracks had an interesting appearance containing dry, damp and wet areas.

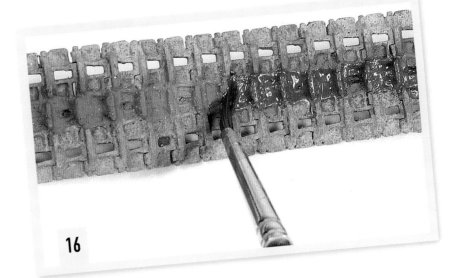

PHOTO 17 AND 18:
The techniques needed for creating the polished steel effects on the outer edges of the cleats will depend on the types of tracks that you are using. On plastic types it is best to rub graphite over these outer surfaces using your finger.

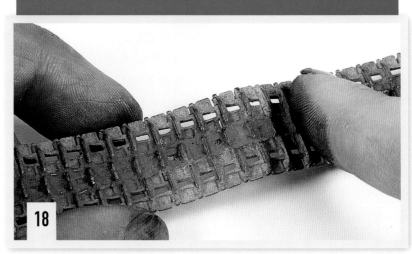

ADDING EARTH TONES AND EFFECTS

» PHOTO 19 THROUGH 21:
The polished effects on the inner parts of the track caused by the road wheels and return rollers were first marked with a pencil then subtly blended using a piece of paper towel.

PHOTO 22 AND 23:
Now it was time to assemble the finished runs of track. I removed the paint from the inner parts of the links using a hobby knife. Removing the paint allowed for open areas of plastic in which to firmly glue the runs together. Slicing away the paint also made it easier to interlock the runs during assembly. Gluing the front run first, which wrapped around the idler, allowed me to properly locate that lower run under the road wheels.

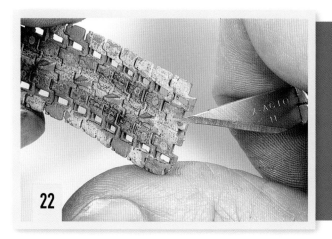

PHOTO 24 THROUGH 26:
Drops of super glue were applied onto the bottom of each road wheel in order to properly fasten them to the track. You will need to apply some pressure to the tops of the wheels for four to five minutes in order to let the glue dry ensuring that all of the wheels are realistically sitting on the track. After, you can fit and glue the remaining runs of track in the way that you feel comfortable. I recommend that you loosen the drive sprocket helping to insure its proper location when assebling the upper and rear smaller sections of track.

Like the hull, tracks should also be weathered in layers ensuring an authentic finish to these important details. As I have shown, it is best to paint plastic tracks in sections separate from the model in order to effectively apply each coat of paint and other effects. Plastic track such as the ones in this example are the most difficult to assemble, finish and attach to a model because they are not flexible or workable. Next we will finish a set of the classic flexible plastic style tracks. Despite the many more accurate alternatives available to us today these tracks are sometimes still preferred by AFV modellers.

24

25

26

WEATHERING RUBBER BAND TYPE TRACKS

ALTHOUGH A MORE COMMON ITEM FOUND IN OLDER KITS, FLEXIBLE PLASTIC TRACKS, REFERRED TO BY MODELLERS AS "RUBBER BAND" TYPE TRACKS, CAN STILL BE A GOOD OPTION WHEN BUILDING AN ARMOUR MODEL.

The ones included in recent kit releases are actually not too bad. This was rather different with the rubber band tracks found in some of the older kits as they were often rather limited in both detail and accuracy.

There are a few advantages to using some of the newer better detailed rubber band tracks. They are quick and easy to assemble with sometimes little or no cleaning required. The AFV-club T-49 tracks that I used on this Sherman, although a bit thick, contained sufficient detail.

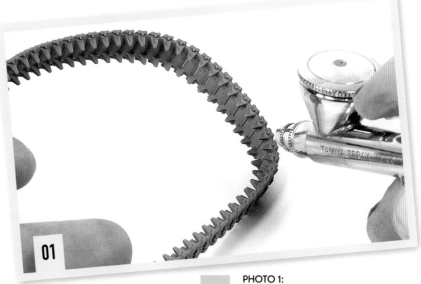

PHOTO 1:

Rubber band tracks are rather easy to paint. After attaching the two ends of each run together I applied a matt earth base coat mixed from acrylic paints. No priming was necessary.

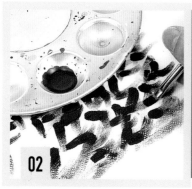

PHOTO 2 THROUGH 4:

On this example I decided to max a dark steel colour using acrylic paints and dry-brushed it onto all of the inner and outer areas where worn steel would be present.

PHOTO 5 AND 6:

I mixed a thick earth coloured slurry from Tamiya paints and plaster. I applied dust coloured pigments for added tone and texture. I added water to slightly to soften the mix. Next I applied it onto the track using an old brush.

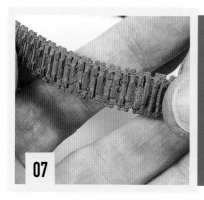

07

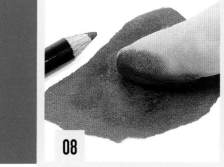

08

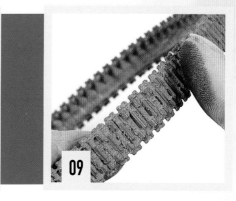

09

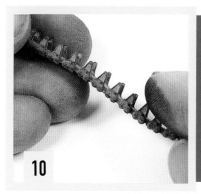

10

11

12

PHOTO 7 THROUGH 10:

I used my finger to wipe the mix from the outer edges of the cleats while it was still wet insuring that these areas would be smooth for the worn steel effects. Graphite was then rubbed over these areas to work in conjunction with the brown metallic colour creating the appearance of worn steel.

PHOTO 11 AND 12:

After locating the tracks onto the model and assembling the armoured side plates I mixed a darker damp earth tone from enamels, oils, pigments and an enamel gloss. I applied this mix to the visible front and rear areas of the track first by brush then with speckling.

13

PHOTO 13 AND 14:

Random wet effects were used to finish the tracks giving me a realistic multi-textured surface of matt, satin and wet areas of mud.

Rubber band type tracks can still be a reasonable option depending on the subject. They assemble quickly and are rather easy to paint.

14

WEATHERING FRAGILE WORKABLE PLASTIC TRACK

MODELKASTEN OFFERS A SERIES OF FINE INJECTION MOLDED WORKABLE TRACK LINK SETS.

Although delicate and time consuming to assemble, Modelkasten sets have a reputation of being very accurate. Many modellers prefer them over other types of after-market track sets.

Assembled sets of Modelkasren track links are very delicate and can sometimes fall apart rather easily when you are handling and painting them. As a result, careful approaches when painting and weathering these and other types of delicate track sets must be taken. You will see that most of the techniques used in this example are much like the ones discussed in the previous two cases. Let's look at this example containing a set for the 12.8cm SfL/61 that I used on this Trumpeter KV 3001 (H).

 PHOTO 1 THROUGH 4:
I painted on a matt earth toned base coat I mixed a slurry from Tamiya paints, pigments and plaster. After thinning the mix using tap water I applied a light coat over the tracks using an old paint brush and quick bursts of air from my airbrush. Keep the coats light when adding the mud effects. If the dried coat is too thick the tracks will fall apart once you try to move the links.

 PHOTO 5 AND 6:
After applying the slurry and letting it dry I carefully bent each link ensuring that the runs of track were still movable. You should perform this task after the application of each technique. Not doing so may cause the layers of paint to build up between the links causing them to fall apart as you try to locate and position them around the model's running gear. The excess dry mix of slurry was wiped away using a paper towel.

 PHOTO 7:
On this example only pigments were used to give extra earth tones to the inner parts of the track. I used light amounts of thinner to blend the pigments. Another thing to remember when using delicate plastic track sets is that small fine parts of plastic can be softened by strong thinners causing them to come loose.

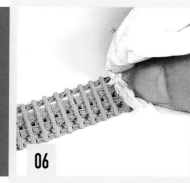

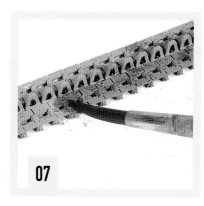

PHOTO 8 AND 9:

A light, damp, mud colour mixed from Humbrol enamel paints, pigments for texture, and gloss was lightly applied for added earth tones and texture. I immediately blended the mix using light amounts of turpentine before it could dry. I also removed the enamel mix from the outer edges of the cleats keeping these parts smooth for the worn steel effects.

PHOTO 10 AND 11:

A metallic tone mixed from Humbrol paints was lightly dry-brushed over the outer edges of the cleats. Graphite was rubbed over the cleats to tone down the bright finish while adding more of a metallic sheen onto these effects.

PHOTO 12 AND 13:

As demonstrated earlier a large artists pencil was used to lightly mark the worn steel effects on the interior parts of the track. This time I blended the pencil marks using a rubber tipped artists shaper. After, the tracks were carefully assembled onto the model.

The two important things to remember when painting sets of delicate Modelkasten track are the following:

1. Always ensure that the tracks are still functional after each coat of paint and any other effects that you may decide to add. Not doing this will allow coats of paint to build up causing the links to fall apart when you try to position them around the models running gear.

2. Always use small amounts of enamel thinners when blending the different effects. Too much thinner may cause the fine plastic parts to come loose resulting in the runs of track falling apart.

Let's now move on to one more example using workable Friulmodel metal tracks.

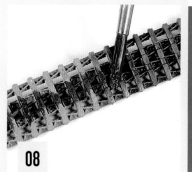

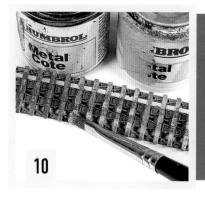

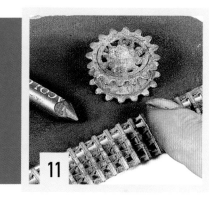

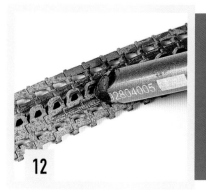

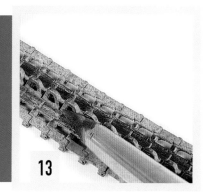

PAINTING TECHNIQUES FOR WORKABLE METAL TRACKS

I PREFER FRIULMODEL WHITE METAL ALLOY TRACK SETS BECAUSE THEY ARE FAIRLY EASY TO ASSEMBLE, HEAVY AND WORKABLE.

I also favour them because they are strong and easy to paint. You can simply lay Friulmodel tracks flat across the table, paint them, and then wrap the runs around the running gear of the model. You can also apply thick coats of mud and other effects over runs of Friulmodel track and they will still work without falling apart. For this example I will be using a product called Quick Rust instead of a basecoat. This water based chemical blend reacts with the surface of the white metal causing it to oxidize. The dark rusty surface that results makes a good initial coat for much of the weathering steps already discussed in the last three examples.

01

PHOTO 1 AND 2:
To oxidize these runs of E-50 tracks I needed a bowl for the Quickrust, a set of tweezers and an old toothbrush. I pulled a few of the wire pins out of the runs of track breaking them down into sections that could easily fit into the bowl.

02

PHOTO 3 AND 4:
After placing a section into the solution I quickly shook them back and forth using the tweezers. You will notice that the tracks will start to turn brown immediately. A brush will be needed to remove air bubbles trapped inside of the treads. I would recommend keeping each of the sections in the solution for about 15 seconds.

03

04

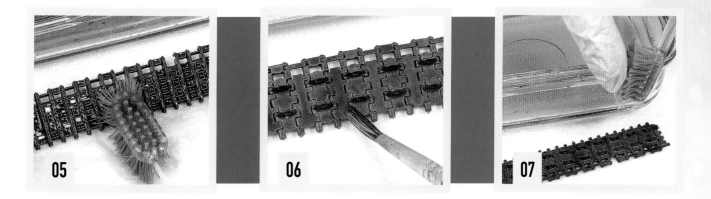

PHOTO 5 THROUGH 7:
After removing the section you can also use an old toothbrush dampened with Quick Rust to brush more of the solution into the treads where air bubbles might have been trapped.

After letting the track sit for a few minutes you can sometimes create more rust tones by applying additional amounts of the Quick Rust.

PHOTO 8 AND 9:
You might still see some patches of white metal where the solution did not reach. You can rub these places using a toothpick dampened with the Quick Rust. One of the metals that make up the white metal alloy will sometimes react with the Quick Rust leaving what looks like random fine layers of salt on the rusty surface. Some of this salt can be removed using a stiff brush.

PHOTO 10:
I now have a nice rusty brown basecoat. Next I reassembled the sections of track. I could start adding the earth tones at this point or apply some more rust tones.

PHOTO 11 THROUGH 13:
I applied some additional corrosion tones by airbrushing random light coats of acrylics and then speckling enamels.

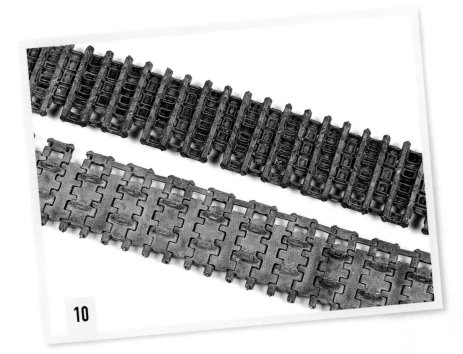

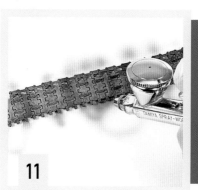

PHOTO 14 AND 15:

The techniques that I used to weather these two sets of track will be more of a review of the steps seen in the previous parts of this chapter so I will be brief with my descriptions. I started by brushing some random tones of pigments onto the tracks and blended them using enamel thinner.

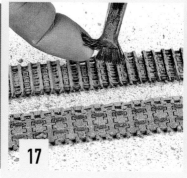

PHOTO 16 THROUGH 18:

A thick slurry made from Tamiya paints, pigments and Plaster of Paris thinned with water was brushed over the exterior of the track. Additional amounts of the same slurry were then speckled for additional texture. After the slurry had time to dry I chipped away the access while at the same time adding more texture using a stiff-bristled brush.

PHOTO 19 THROUGH 21:

Darker satin earth tones mixed from brown Humbrol enamel, pigments and a gloss varnish were randomly brushed on the track and blended.

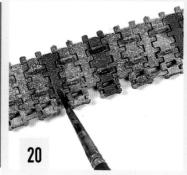

PHOTO 22 AND 23:

Next an enamel gloss was used to add some wet areas.

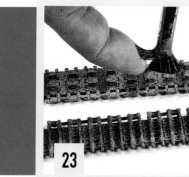

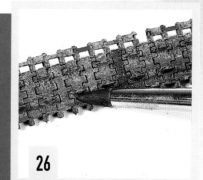
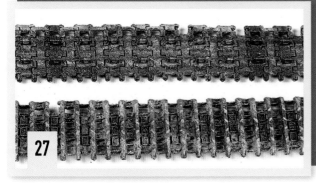

PHOTO 24 THROUGH 28:
The outer sides of the track were polished using sandpaper to expose the white metal on the raised cleats. The polished metallic inner sides of the tracks where obtained using a large pencil then blended using a rubber tipped artist sharpener.

At this point we have covered four examples for weathering tracks. Most of the paints and methods used are the same as the ones applied to the rest of the model. Sometimes these techniques can vary as to how fragile the tracks are, if they are workable or not and what they are made from. Tracks should be weathered in layers like the rest of the AFV to ensure that they are both authentic and interesting to look at. Let's continue with some examples of adding heavy dust and thick layers of earth onto a model.

HEAVY DUST AND THICK LAYERS OF EARTH

THICK LAYERS OF DUST AND MUD CAN REALLY ADD A LOT OF CHARACTER TO A VEHICLE.

Viewing photos of both WWII and modern AFVs will show that large amounts of dust and earth, depending on the environment and theater of operations, would often quickly adhere to these vehicles. Thick layers of mud can really give another interesting level of effects in conjunction with the other weathering. These thick coats of earth need to be built up in layers in order to look natural.

In this part we are going to look at two examples of how to build up heavy dust and thick layers of earth. The first example over a winter Tiger I will be more of a normal instance. In the second example we will be continuing the weathering of the LVT-(A) by applying heavy coats of wet mud and beach sand.

You will observe that much of the techniques we will be using to build up heavy dust and thick layers of earth have already been discussed throughout the past chapters. Let's get going with our first example.

BUILT UP LAYERS OF MUD

THICK BUILT UP LAYERS OF MUD, WHEN PROPERLY APPLIED ONTO A MODEL, ARE ACTUALLY NOT THAT SUBSTANTIAL.

In fact these effects when done correctly will not really hide as much of the fine details as you might think. You now have seen that weathering is most authentic when done in different layers containing areas of matt, satin and glossy textures. This could not be truer for thick layers of mud. The first steps in this segment were demonstrated earlier so they will be more of a review. Let's start by again quickly looking at the first weathering steps that are needed to act as a base for the heavier effects applied after.

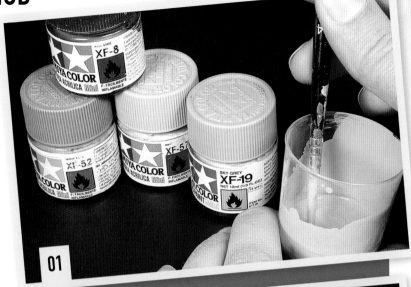

**PHOTO 1 THROUGH 3:**

I started with a base coat of dust mixed from Tamiya paints. A small amount of blue was added to the mix. The blue would help give a feeling of damp coldness to the completed model as it was depicted to be in a cold winter setting. Light amounts of the dust mix were randomly airbrushed over different parts of the hull turret and running gear. Remember to use this step to also help create contrast between parts.

04

PHOTO 4:
Rainmarks were also applied to the sides of the hull, turret and fenders using an earth tone mixed form the same four Tamiya colors, this time diluted with water. This step was also used to add more random dust effects to the upper parts of the turret and hull.

PHOTO 5 THROUGH 7:
Four different pigment colors were blended over the dust tones created with the Tamiya colors in the previous step. An enamel thinner was used to blend the pigments.

05

06

07

PHOTO 8:
As a result of the missing fenders I knew that large amounts of mud would be present on the rear of the hull. I started building up these areas using the pigments over the Tamiya earth tones airbrushed before.

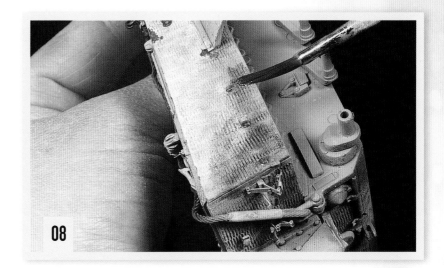

PHOTO 9:
During this time dry dark earth toned pigments were brushed around some of the details such as the front driver's visor to create contrast amongst these parts and the rest of the hull.

PHOTO 10 THROUGH 12:
I added some grey to the same earth tone mixed back in photo one darkening it a bit. A fine coat of this darker earth tone was airbrushed onto the shadowed under sides of the hull and inner wheels of the running gear.

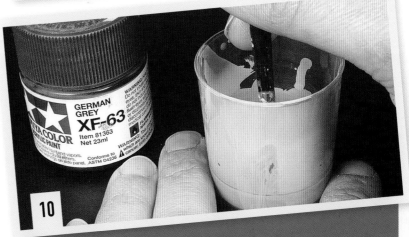

PHOTO 13 THROUGH 15:

I mixed my reliable slurry as demonstrated throughout this chapter using Tamiya paints, pigments, plaster and tap water. I added this mix onto the hull rear with a brush and quick bursts of air from my airbrush further building up the mud tones. Once dry, a modified stiff bristled brush was used to remove some of the excess texture that was out of scale giving the dry earth more of a convincing surface. Just lightly rub the stiff bristled brush and some of the texture of the dry slurry will simply crumble away.

PHOTO 16 THROUGH 18:

More of the slurry was applied to the wheels using an old paint brush and quick bursts of air from my airbrush. Note the homemade jig constructed from sheet plastic used to keep the wheels from being blown across the table durring this step. Once more I removed some of the excess texture using a modified stiff bristled brush.

PHOTO 19 AND 20:

More of the slurry was brushed onto the outer diameter of some of the wheels. Next I pressed the wheel onto a flat surface to flatten the slurry. We will discuss why this was done momentarily.

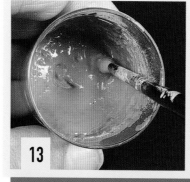

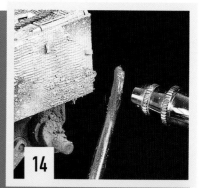

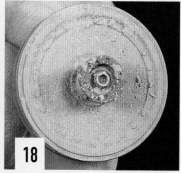

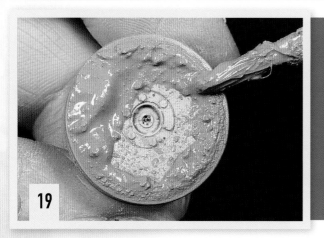

PHOTO 21 AND 22:
A dark damp earth tone was mixed using a brown enamel, oil paint, pigments and a gloss varnish. The darker tone was applied randomly over the lighter earth areas on the hull and running gear, again using quick bursts of air from my airbrush.

PHOTO 23 THROUGH 25:
This damp earth tone was also brushed onto the outer edges of some of the road wheels and subtly blended using enamel thinner. More damp earth was also applied to the upper hull and also blended. Remember that you can use this step to create even more contrast between details on the upper parts of the model.

Although some of the fine details were covered on the running gear and lower hull it cannot be denied that the heavy earth tones contribute greatly to the imposing look of this winter veteran Tiger I. The layers of mud help give the viewer a feeling as to the damp rough environment in which this vehicle operated giving more of a historical sense to the model.

You can also see how the airbrushed dust tones, dry earth slurry and enamel damp earth mixes all work together giving a multi-textured authentic looking coat of weathering effects to the model. Note how the dark damp earth tones were painted mostly onto the wheels of the vehicle giving life to the running gear that makes up a very large part of the models surface. The thick mud that we pressed in photo 20 represents the terrain that has been pushed smooth on the inner wheels by the the outer overlapping ones.

Like with the wet effects in the previous chapters note how the damp enamel mix was also applied to parts of the upper hull and turret then blended with turpentine. As on the running gear this damp earth will help to break up the dry lighter coloured dust tones while also adding more of a damp cold look to the model. With all of this in mind lets look at another example of heavy weathering on the LVT-(A) 1.

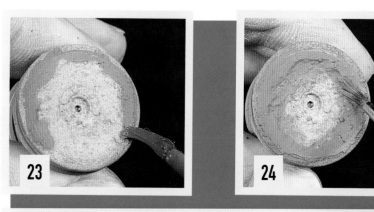

THICK WET LAYERS OF MUD

LET'S MOVE ON WITH THE LVT-(A) 1 THAT WE STARTED WEATHERING EARLIER IN THIS BOOK WHEN APPLYING THE DUST TONES AND RAINMARKS

On this example we are going to continue with using some different approaches for obtaining layers of thick wet mud on an AFV in a tropical setting. Again some of the steps will contain techniques that will be more of a review.

PHOTO 1 THROUGH 4:
I started by applying a light earth slurry mixed from Tamiya paints, pigments and plaster using the speckling technique. I removed the excessive over scale texture using a few dry clean paintbrushes. Use a downward motion when removing the texture on the sides of the hull.

01

02

03

04

PHOTO 5 THROUGH 8:
I needed to build up layers of earth under the tracks. I did this by piling up bits of pigments and applying tiny amounts of fixer using a pipette. I needed to repeat this step two to three times until I obtained the result in photo eight.

PHOTO 9 THROUGH 11:

I continued to add more light earth by speckling using the same slurry applied in photo one to add more texture onto the built up mud. I also decided to speckle more of the slurry around the insides behind the tracks, onto the lower road wheels and onto the outer sides where large amounts of earth would fall due to the angled mud hopper. Again I removed some of the unwanted clumps of texture with a vertical motion using a dry brush.

PHOTO 12 THROUGH 14:

I decided to brush more of the earth toned slurry over the built up pigments after they had about 24 hours or so to set. I also used this earth mix to apply vertical streaks under the mud guards. Again, part of the Tamiya pigment plaster mix was removed using a vertical sweeping motion with a dry clean paint brush.

PHOTO 15 THROUGH 17:
For added earth tones I painted on a darker mud colour mixed from an enamel brown, earth coloured pigments and artist oils, then blended it using enamel thinner.

After, I thinned the enamel mix and speckled it over the layers of thick mud and onto the running gear.

 PHOTO 18 THROUGH 20:
I blended some more of the dark earth mix onto the sides more toward the rear of the vehicle. Dark earth streaks were also blended under the mud guards. The tracks were placed onto the model at this time.

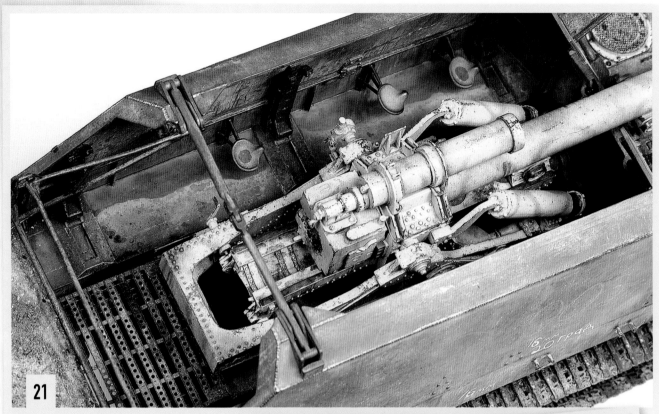

PHOTO 21 THROUGH 23:
One of the key weathering traits to this LVT finish are the wet effects. I have said earlier in this book that wet glossy effects can break up your matt earth tones while adding contrast to areas and details. The large wet effects added to the interior of this rusty matt Geschuzwagen Tiger Fur 17cm added a whole different texture making this photo more interesting. These wet effects and much of the ones on this LVT were applied using an enamel gloss right out of the bottle with a little thinner in order to make it a bit easier to apply. Most of the wet effects applied to this model were made from a mix of about four parts enamel gloss and one part thinner.

PHOTO 24 THROUGH 26:
The fairly dry T-64 exhaust in photo 24 surrounded by the darker moist mud on the fender is a great example as to how damp earth and wet effects can add contrast between parts and details. On the LVT contrast was created between the small and large plates on the upper front hull using wet effects making this rather featureless part of the model much more appealing. Speckling more of the gloss mix over these panels helped to subtly unify the wet effects making the effect more natural.

PHOTO 27 AND 28:
Vallejo Still Water was used to give a very wet saturated appearance to the thick layers of mud. This mix was also brushed onto the track making them look equally as wet.
Make sure that your tracks are attached onto the model if you are going to give them a coat of Vallejo Still Water. Although it took the Vallejo Still Water four or five hours to dry the tracks were unmovable once it had solidified.

ADDING EARTH TONES AND EFFECTS **210**

PHOTO 29 AND 30:
I returned to using the enamel gloss to add the rest of the runs on the sides of the model.

The areas of thick mud and wet effects are two of the primary features that make this model look both realistic and unique. The chipping, colour modulation and other effects also play an important role in the model's completed appearance, but the earth tones will certainly work as one of the quick eye catching features drawing attention to the piece. With this LVT and the Tiger I, I have demonstrated how heavy weathering can give the modeller another level of creativity for adding life and originality to their a replica.

This part will complete this chapter on adding earth tones and effects. Although the largest chapter in this book there are still a few effects that I will demonstrate in the remaining parts that will further enhance the appearance of your finished model. In the next chapter we will look at techniques for finishing steel road wheels.

14 PAINTING STEEL ROAD WHEELS

I USUALLY WAIT UNTIL AFTER MOST OF THE WEATHERING IS COMPLETED TO PAINT STEEL ROAD WHEELS.

These details are usually smooth and polished. The methods that I use to finish these parts are rather simple.

PHOTO 1 THROUGH 4:

After the weathering steps I remove the paint and clean the outer surfaces of the wheels using sandpaper. The first step in creating the polished steel effects on these edges is to apply a few coats of an aluminum coloured Humbrol enamel. First wipe the excess paint away from the flat brush onto a piece of paper. Some of the colour might overflow onto the sides of the wheels if you have too much paint on the brush creating an unrealistic result. Graphite from a pencil was then rubbed over the aluminum colour to tone it down a bit while also adding a shinny metallic glare to the surface.

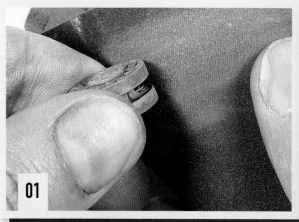

05

PHOTO 5 AND 6:
Creating the polished metallic edges on the outer diameters of these white metal JS-3 road wheels produced by Friulmodel was rather easy. I simply sanded the paint away from the outer edges of these details revealing the metallic surface underneath, much like the outers cleats on the tracks shown in the previous chapter.

06

15 SIMULATING OIL, GREASE AND SPLIT FUEL

OIL, GREASE AND SPILT FUEL ARE INTERESTING EFFECTS THAT ARE ALWAYS FUN TO APPLY.

These effects, along with all of the other weathering, help to give a gritty feeling of both usage and history to a model. The sleek, darker grease effects on this Geschuzwagen Tiger Fur 17cm stabilization foot contrast very nicely with the lighter matt rusty finish of the steel.

This section has been broken down into two parts. The first is entitled, "Oil and Grease" and the second is called "Spilt Fuel". Each of the sections will contain a number of examples of how and where to apply these effects. Let's now continue.

OIL AND GREASE

HERE WE ARE GOING TO LOOK AT SOME METHODS FOR APPLYING GREASE AND OIL EFFECTS.

You should remember that authentic grease and oil stains usually contain both satin and glossy areas. Dust adheres to of fresh grease so these effects should usually have earth tones present.

Today there are pre-mixed products on the market from different companies to help modellers quickly apply basic grease and oil effects. Of course some people still prefer to mix their own and there are a number of different mediums that can be used. Most of the time grease and oil effects are applied after much of the weathering steps. I will start by showing a few typical ways to place these effects over earth tones. The last example will need a few more steps as I apply some large grease runs to break up the side of a rather clean T-34 hull.

>> **PHOTO 1 THROUGH 3:**
The pre-mixed effects available on the market are probably the quickest way to apply basic oil and grease effects. First shake the bottle well making sure that all of the pigments have been thoroughly mixed.

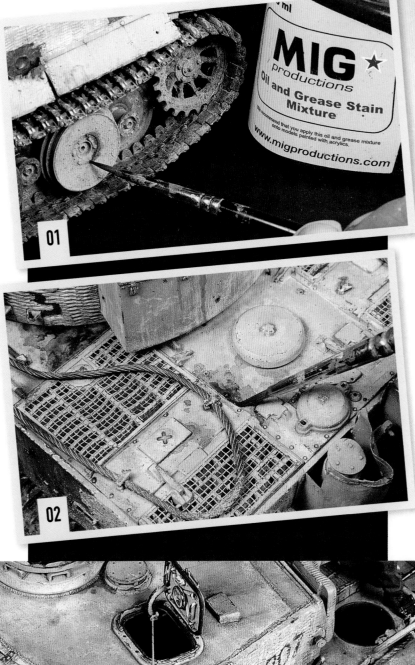

01

02

03

PHOTO 4 THROUGH 8:

The oil effects applied to this JSU-152 were simply mixed using brown and black oil paints. Enamel gloss was also added and the whole mix was then diluted with thinner. You can apply the mix on in thick opaque amounts then blend it. More diluted amounts can also be brushed on as a wash such as I added around the hubs of the road wheels.

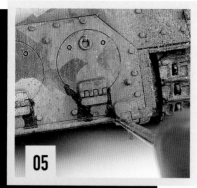

PHOTO 9 AND 10:

The rails and wheels for the recoil of this 17cm cannon required a different approach. First I brushed a light grey tone over what would be the polished areas using acrylics. Next I rubbed a few layers of graphite over the grey tones.

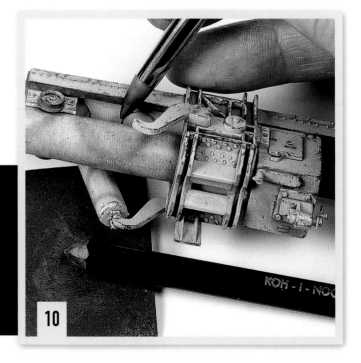

PHOTO 11 THROUGH 13:
A random coat consisting of some thinned enamel gloss with a dark grey pigment finished the grease areas.

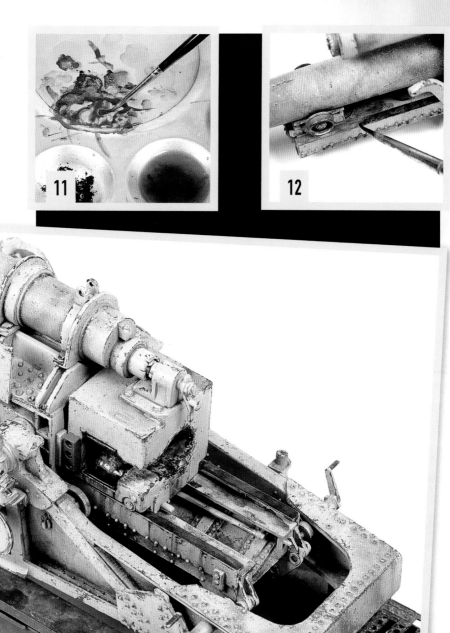

11

12

13

PHOTO 14 THROUGH 16:
In the case of the suspension on this LVT a brown enamel was mixed with some enamel gloss and some dark grey pigments. The mix was then diluted and applied as a thick wash in specific areas where fresh grease would be present. Not being totally content with the semi-satin finish of these effects I decided to apply some Tamiya smoke to increase the glossiness around the center of the hub.

14

15

16

17

18

PHOTO 17 THROUGH 20:

For this Geschuzwagen Tiger a very viscous wash of brown enamels, dark grey pigments and gloss varnish was mixed. The thinned mix was placed randomly at different intensities around the perimeter of the large plate located on the upper hull. Tamiya smoke was then applied randomly over the dark grey satin wash after it had dried for a bit mostly into the seam in order to obtain random glossy regions in the grease effects.

19

20

PHOTO 21 AND 22:

You can observe in this example how grease and oil effects can be used to help distinguish these two plates from each other. You can also see that these grease stains, visible at different intensities, contain authentic glossy and satin regions. The grease effects were applied onto some of the road wheels in the same manner giving realistic fresh glossy and older satin regions.

21

22

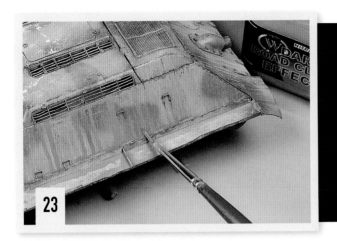

PHOTO 23 THROUGH 25:
I wanted to apply a rather large grease affect to break up the side of this T-34. Dust effects should usually be present around grease effects and this area contained only light weathering. For the first step I brushed on some enamel earth effects then blended them using thinner. Next I added some darker enamel earth effects in the same manner to create light variations in the tones.

PHOTO 26 AND 27:
Wet runs were added using thinned amounts of enamel gloss. More wet effects were applied using the speckling technique to subtly unify the runs.

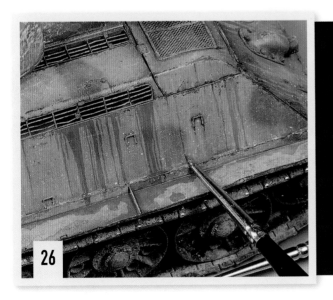

PHOTO 28 THROUGH 31:

After letting the earth and wet effects dry I continued by adding some opaque satin oil runs mixed from a dark enamel matt grey and some gloss. The mix was diluted with thinner. I applied some light earth pigments to blend the edges of the stains on the fenders.

PHOTO 32 AND 33:

I mixed a glossy semi transparent tone using Tamiya smoke with just a bit of hull red. I airbrushed the tone over the dark grease runs, under the grill and onto the fenders. Airbrushing the glossy semi-transparent Tamiya mix in this manner made the grease effects look as though they had been absorbed by the capillary action of the dust.

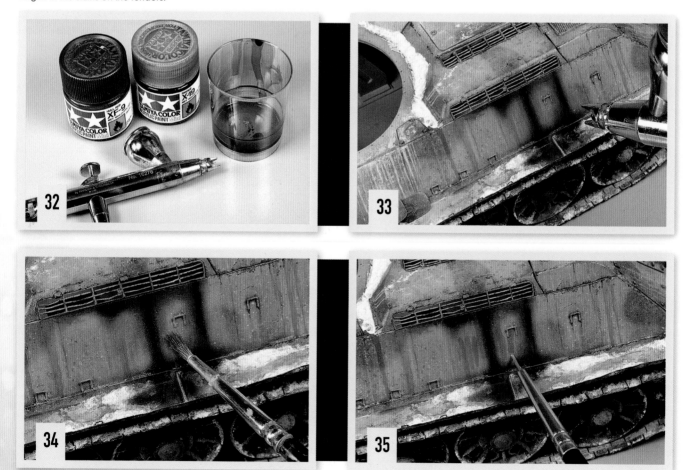

PHOTO 34 THROUGH 36:
I finished by applying some more dust toned pigments around the runs of grease and blending them with enamel thinner.

These are all examples of the various techniques and different mediums that I use to apply areas of oil and grease. Remember that these effects, when applied creatively, can also create contrast amongst parts such as on the upper hull plate of

the Geschuzwagen Tiger or simply break up large flat surfaces like on the side of the T-34/122. Also remember that where there is grease and oil dust effects should also be present. Let's look at a few examples of creating spilt fuel effects.

The snow on the running gear in this photo was created using product from the WILDER line called "Textured Snow".

SPILT FUEL

SPILT FUEL EFFECTS ARE MUCH LIKE OIL AND GREASE IN THAT THEY USUALLY COINCIDE WITH DUST

 PHOTO 1 AND 2:
The spilt fuel effects added to the cylindrical fuel tank of the JS-3 were rather easy to make. I started with a light airbrushed coat of dust mixed from acrylics. Tape was used because the effects in my reference photo had a rather straight edge on one side while the opposite was more blended. Next a layer of pigments was applied over the base of light earth..

PHOTO 3 THROUGH 5:
A transparent brown tone mixed from gloss enamels and artist oils was used to finish the effect.

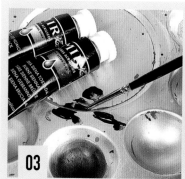

PHOTO 6 THROUGH 8:
The method I used to apply the fuel stains on this LVT was pretty much the same as on the JS-3 accept Tamiya clear paints were used in place of the oils and enamel gloss. To start, a satin coat of fresh sand was mixed using a matt brown enamel and some gloss diluted with a little thinner.

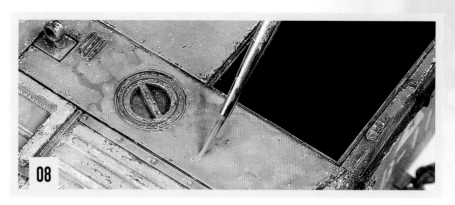

08

09

PHOTO 9 THROUGH 11:
An orange fresh fuel tone was mixed using Tamiya clear colors that I thinned into a wash using lacquer thinner. You need to be careful and quick when applying spilt fuel effects in this manner. Lacquer thinner is a strong solvent and will quickly attack the base coat if you manipulate the paint for too long in one area.

The T-72 is an example of how areas of spilt fuel can help to add contrast between details. It is simple to see the external fuel tank that sticks out from the others on the fender. Spilt fuel effects are easy to apply and can help to give life to a scale model while also giving us one more way to create contrasting parts.

10

11

16 EXHAUST AND SMOKE EFFECTS

EXHAUST AND SMOKE EFFECTS ARE FAIRLY UNCOMPLICATED TO PAINT.

Though I paint the exhaust pipes prior to adding any earth tones, I usually wait until after the weathering steps are completed before applying any smoke effects. I usually start by carefully airbrushing the smoke effects using a

matt black acrylic then brush on some black pigments over these areas. Sometimes I will add light amounts of blue and oxide colors to the black when creating diesel exhaust effects. Let's go over a few examples.

01

PHOTO 1:
For the first example we will be painting diesel exhaust effects like the ones seen on the rear of this Soviet SU-100 onto the JSU-152.

PHOTO 2 AND 3:
I airbrushed a coat of matt black Tamiya paint onto the areas around the opening of the armoured exhaust

covers. Light amounts of black pigments were brushed over the Tamiya paint helping to create a further authentic matt effect.

02

03

PHOTO 4 AND 5:

Bits of a dark maroon tone representing left over oil and other impurities from the low-quality diesel fuel were applied using the speckling technique. I made this tone using a blend of black, blue, brown and gloss enamels mixed with pigments. The pigments provided a bit of texture to the blend. Like with the T-34 on the other page note the satin texture of oil and other impurities around the exhaust of this T-55 recovery vehicle

PHOTO 6 AND 7:

I added some more runs of oil using the same dark maroon tone finishing the effect.

08

09

PHOTO 8 AND 9:
The techniques used to produce the smoke effects on the gun of this JSU-152 were pretty much the same. I airbrushed a very light coat of black around the openings of the muzzle break. In this case I used acrylic paints from a tube thinned with tap water. Pigments were again used to touch up the black areas helping to create a realistic matt smoke appearance. Please note that only very faint smoke effects are often needed on muzzle breaks such as in this example.

10

PHOTO 10:
The effects around the exhaust pipes for this gasoline driven Geschuzwagen Tiger Fur 17cm were rather subtle. Note that other then on the very tip of the opening only a little black has been applied to the exterior of the pipe. If you look at reference pictures such as the T-34 in photo number one you will see that very little soot is present on the external surface of exhaust pipes.

PHOTO 11 THROUGH 15:
In the case of this Tiger I covered the protectors over the openings of the exhausts using a liquid mask before I airbrushed the interiors black. I very carefully peeled the mask away revealing the tops of the protectors, airbrushed a bit more matt black around the perimeters, and then brushed on some pigments to finish the effects.

The exhaust and smoke effects are usually one of the last touches that I add to a model. Impacts are another detail that I save until the end. Let's move on to an example of painting impacts.

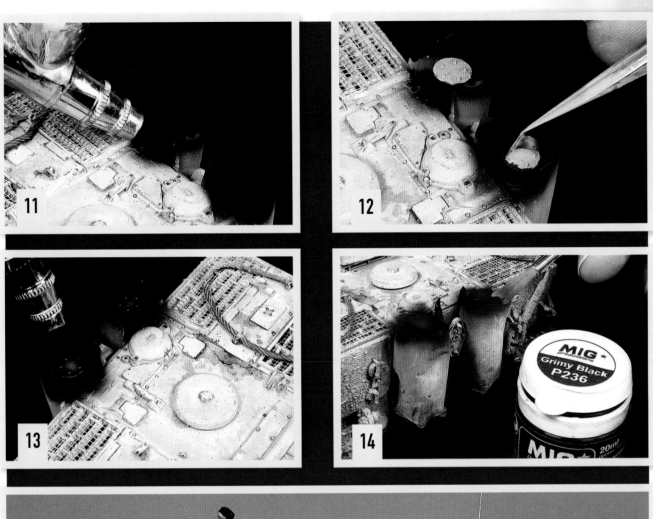

17 PAINTING IMPACTS

IMPACTS ARE USAULY ONE OF THE FINAL THINGS THAT I FINISH WHEN PAINTING A VEHICLE.

Nicely painted impacts are really interesting details that work together with other damaged effects to help give character and a bit of history to an armour model. Let's finish these impacts on this Tiger I

PHOTO 1 THROUGH 3 :

I began by carefully airbrushing each of the strikes and the areas around them using matt brown acrylics. Next I airbrushed a medium rust tone onto the impacts. A very heavy rust wash of thinned oil paints mixed with pigments was applied to add more tones over the brown and rust acrylics.

PHOTO 4 THROUGH 6:

As the rust wash was drying I mixed a faded sand tone, a brown steel colour and a lighter dull oxide primer shade. Using a very fine 000 brush I painted fine flakes and chips caused by the heat of the strikes onto the oxide primer and dark yellow areas.

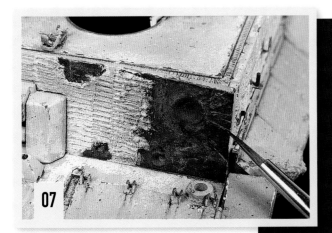

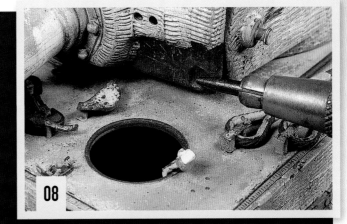

PHOTO 7 THROUGH 9:

I mixed a light grey shade from oil paints and randomly painted subtle streaks caused from red hot bits of flying metal around some of the impacts. The final touch was to add some metallic tones onto the perimeter of the impacts.

You can see that the numerous impacts work in conjunction with the other damage and weathering effects to help create a convincing replica. I always recommend applying impacts onto heavy armour. They are very enjoyable details to create.

SIMULATING WORN STEEL
WORN PAINTED STEEL IS A PLEASING, EASY EFFECT TO CREATE.

It's a simple, subtle technique that gives your model a faint shiny look of actual metal. I demonstrated some examples of simulating worn steel back in chapter 11 about painting exterior components. It should be applied after the weathering effects. The thinners used to blend earth toned enamels and pigments, for example, will reduce this important effect. This technique is achieved by simply rubbing graphite over specific parts of a model where the paint has been worn away. You can apply the graphite using a pencil or with your finger as you have already seen.

01

PHOTO 2 THROUGH 7 :
These photos display five examples for some of the places where I usually rub graphite to simulate metallic areas noticeable through worn paint. Note that these areas are in places where lots of chipping is present. Another good place where worn satin steel would be present is on the corners of the superstructure and fenders. Graphite should also be rubbed around hatches due to the crew entering and exiting the vehicle. Simulating worn steel is the last effect that I add before finishing a scale armour model. In the case of this JSU I only needed to permanently glue the parts such as the 152 gun assembly and the DShK in place.

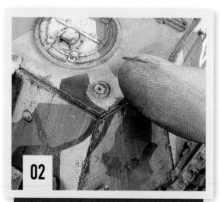

02

PHOTO 1 :
In the photo above we see the suspension of a T-26 resting at the Parola Museum in Finland. This is a good example of paint being worn away over time revealing polished metallic areas from the climbing of inquisitive visitors.

03

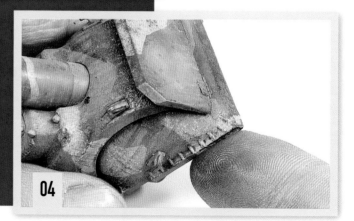

04

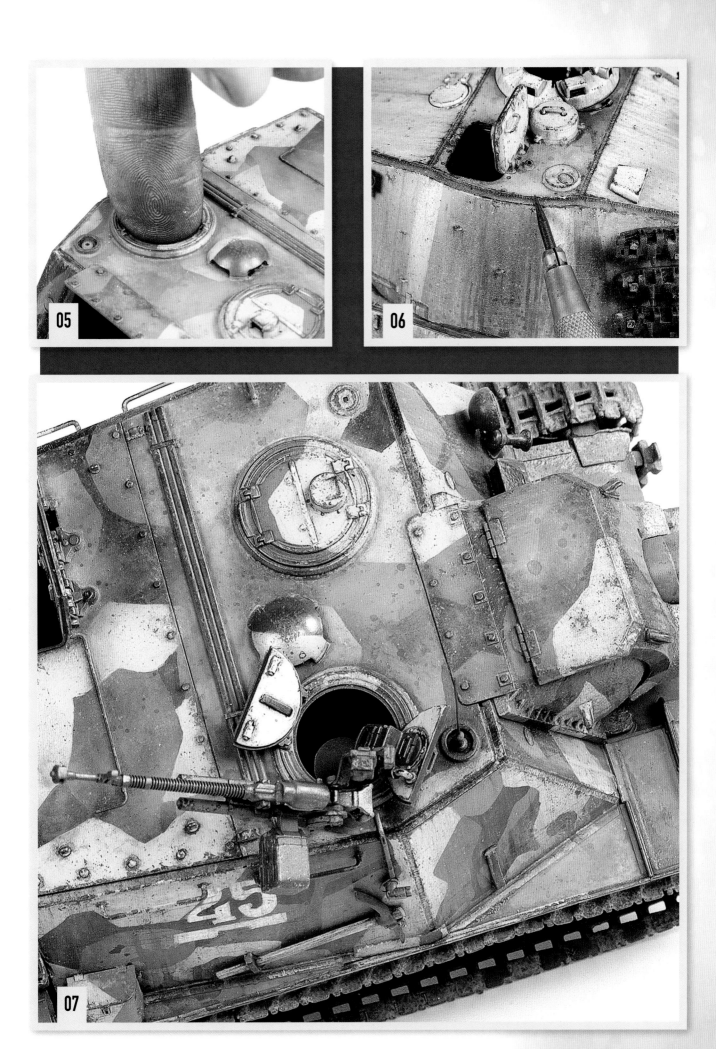